This book is a must-read if...

- you want to read inspirational stories by others;

- you like to read short stories you can dip in and out of as you choose;

- you wish to immerse yourself in personal journeys of discovery;

- you are looking to connect with like-minded men who have experienced what you have;

- you want to be inspired by how others have embraced their vulnerabilities and gone against the status quo;

- you want to be a change-maker and make a difference to the world around you;

- you want to be inspired by people from different walks of life all over the world.

"As a society, we need to encourage men to tell and share their stories. This book does just that.

From tales of overcoming adversity to stories of hope and inspiration, this book would enrich you with the depth of emotion and insight it provides into each individual story. It's a powerful collection of stories from different people, all in just one volume providing something for everyone.

I highly recommend it!"

Adesola Orimalade
Author, Speaker, Transformational Leader

"We all have our own definition of strength. For me, it's about giving yourself the power to overcome obstacles to succeed and to leave a lasting legacy. These truly inspirational stories are proof that when you have purpose, lives can be completely transformed, no matter who you are. Not everyone finds their inner power, so it's heartening and hugely significant to read these individual life changing perspectives from 17 male Voices of Strength. A fabulous idea and written brilliantly."

Aneela Rose
Founder and Managing Director at Rose Media Group,
Motivational Speaker, Team GB Powerlifter

"*Voices of Strength* is a book needed more than ever, especially in current times, to appreciate men who continue to inspire through action, committed to their true masculine energy, which is protective, nurturing, out of the box from restrictive norms and the limiting obsessions for powers, bigotry and misogyny.

These men break the conventional expectations of the illusory definition of male energy, by showcasing strength of character over muscle strength, resilience to walk the talk, respect for life and femininity, and acknowledge the need for change to make the world a place of empathy and kindness, rather than hunger for a seat at the table of power. For them, this is the new narrative and we celebrate these men as leaders who are ever willing to listen, stand for the dignity and honour of femininity and collaborate to make the world a better place where harmony, peace and growth is for all.

Congratulations, Brenda, my dearest sister, for bringing to the world; such inspiring stories through this book."

Ann D'Silva
Author, Activist, Humanitarian

"It takes great courage for a man to go against the tide and find his authentic voice. The stories within *Voices of Strength* clearly illustrate the pivotal moments and events that spurred these men to forge their paths and step into their authentic selves. Their leadership is clear, and they have a message that many others must hear."

Dr P.K.Rajput MBA, Ph.D, FISSAT, FIAECT, MLE^{SM}
Author

VOICES OF STRENGTH

COMPILED BY
BRENDA DEMPSEY

First published in Great Britain in 2023
by Book Brilliance Publishing
265A Fir Tree Road, Epsom, Surrey, KT17 3LF
+44 (0)20 8641 5090
www.bookbrilliancepublishing.com
admin@bookbrilliancepublishing.com

A CIP catalogue record for this book is available
at the British Library.

ISBN 978-1-913770-67-9

Typeset in Garamond.

Articles correct at time of submission.

To the men who have yet to find the courage
to be different, embrace their vulnerabilities
and unapologetically live life on their terms
according to their inner cultivated landscape.

Contents

Foreword

It is a great pleasure to provide an endorsement for such an incredible array of stories, insights, talented authors, and leaders.

When we think about male strength, the picture of Hercules comes to mind; that brute strength is a man who should deal with his feelings or 'man up' as they say. The truth is, to be a man of strength is to live a life of feeling, rather than never being allowed to feel. In the brilliant song by Tears for Fears, *Woman in Chains*, Roland Orzabal refers to the feminine within a man that is held in chains because we are conditioned and conform to think and act like the stereotype of a man. But thankfully, times are changing...

Sometimes we need brute strength, but the real power of strength lies within. It lies within the myriad of being attuned to our very self, our authentic self and our inner resilience to deal with life's fortitudes.

My philosophy steeped in being a survivor of the Hillsborough football tragedy and life experiences – like divorce, illness, injury and grief – requires more profound inner resilience to survive. Without exception, experiencing the joy of life through magical moments of laughter, adventures and exploration with far more good times than bad, I have always needed to find my inner strength and resilience to overcome the challenges and enjoy the rewards. The more character-building moments we have and the more we can expose ourselves to new experiences, the greater our inner character and strength become. And that is why finding your inner voice is essential in this life. Living true to that voice and your authentic self is even more critical, along with understanding your reason for being, because this can give you the greatest inner strength.

Viktor Frankl states in his incredible book, *Man's Search for Meaning*, those who find meaning in their life, no matter how dark their days, are the ones who tend to survive what life throws at them. Furthermore, as Friedrich Nietzsche says, "He who has a why can bear anyhow." One of the building blocks that will provide inner strength is to have meaning in one's life, but what is fantastic about life is that we get to decide.

So, that's why a book like this is so significant in this time of change. Men who share their Voices of Strength, stories and insights help us understand how we can use our inner strength to face what is before us and better understand the power within us.

When you read these stories, you will hear various life lessons. The learning of these lessons will support your ongoing growth, touching your inner self to seek new ways of finding courage and inner strength to help you in those moments of need.

So, take the time to find yourself in this anthology of stories and consider the author's life as you turn each page, focusing on their lessons and meaning to help you define yours.

Enjoy this magnificent edition of stories of strength and always keep smiling...

Paul Corke

Author, Speaker, Thought Leader and Influencer

Introduction

Over the last five years, I have compiled several successful Amazon #1 anthologies. I have achieved this not only as an international #1 bestselling author, but as a publisher too. I embarked on an incredible transformation journey in 2020 when I founded Book Brilliance Publishing during lockdown after people approached me to support them in writing and publishing their books. In the past, my books have focused on women, but in July 2021, I brought together 45 Resilient Voices (male and female), who made Amazon #1 bestseller status on the day of publication, to share their stories borne out of lockdown.

As a publisher, I work with both men and women, and it was through working with men and seeing their transformations that I sparked the idea of compiling powerful stories from a male perspective. Their stories evidenced change within them directly from their experiences and the introspection that ensued. The inner journey is the most significant journey a human can take, and when men embark on this adventure, it transforms them into leading lives from a place of authenticity.

On contemplating a more profound meaning as to why and how I should conduct this project, it led me to research the power of masculine numbers. I wanted to align the book project to angelic numerology as *Voices of Strength* is a book with Soul; therefore, its foundation had to come from a spiritual place.

My research discovered that the number 17 is responsible for insight, responsibility, self-discipline, strength, compassion, spiritual consciousness, wisdom, a desire for peace and love for all of humanity. As you can see, the number 17 is significant and highly spiritual.

My mission involved bringing together 17 male Voices of Strength to show the world the transformational journey men are undertaking because they no longer wish to be part of the status quo. These men have connected within, gained enlightenment from their adversities and are ready to roar their message to the world. These men, fuelled with purpose, know the significance of working collaboratively to make a difference, and are prepared to step into their power and create a ripple effect that the world has never seen before.

By contributing as a co-author, they understand that the platform will increase their visibility, help them to be seen as the author of authority and innovatively grow their brand. Always conscious of how they can further influence, inspire and impact others, they seek ways to share their powerful messages so they can not only be the change-makers but the catalyst for change in the world.

Voices of Strength's intention is a dream come true by bringing like-minded men together by creating a community. Bonds and relationships developed, and the men are already creating further opportunities for collaborations and joint ventures. Anthologies create ripples of Brilliance for the co-authors and readers.

It is time for you to acknowledge their resounding voices as they are heard and understood. Creating this all-male book will illustrate an invigorated energy that is not ego-led but heart-led, which restores balance to the world. It is time to leave your legacy.

I hope *Voices of Strength* inspires you to find your courage, take a leap of faith and follow your gut by being the beacon of light that shines a new path for future generations.

Do Different!

Be Brilliant!

Love
Brenda

Douglas Vermeeren is the epitome of someone with the courage and commitment to follow their heart and dreams. As a multi-talented actor, stuntman, director and producer, Douglas enjoys the fruits of his labour and shares his love with audiences, family and his dedicated team. One attains such high echelons not by chance, but by hard work, belief and passion.

In his chapter, Douglas captures the true essence of a Voice of Strength as he is fearless in sharing his story and using his voice to influence, inspire and impact others to find the courage to make better life choices.

On a cruise, I heard him speak about his love of movies and stunts but, more importantly, his commitment to being the best version of himself through teaching personal development. His words of wisdom are to be heard and acted upon. Enjoy…

Brenda

Douglas Vermeeren

"Everything you do takes courage, but you soon learn to trust that courage will always be there for you."

Douglas Vermeeren

I think the most significant influences for becoming the man I am today in the 21st century have come from my mom and grandmother. Of course, my father was there too, and he had things to teach, but I believe the women in our life are often the more vital teachers.

These two highly influential, strong, powerful women taught me how to associate with other women and people in general. Watching them taught me how to live a life with dignity and respect. The most significant part of that process starts with respecting and having grace for yourself. People have a very public persona of who they are, and their private persona often doesn't match up. You could argue that many people are different when alone, in secret, which I feel conflicts with authentically living your life. The memories I have of this skewed concept are that it was instilled in me to be the best I could be in both public and private situations.

I witnessed first-hand how these two women conducted their lives underpinned by respect for themselves. There's a little saying that I use to reinforce the idea of infusing respect within yourself: "A lifeguard can't save others until they know how to swim." So you need to learn those skills for yourself, and if you can, learn how to be kind to yourself.

One of the challenges people face is learning to be fair about themselves. Learning to look inwards and being honest means sometimes you've got to call it for what it is, and this can be tricky as we always want the best, but sometimes we fall short. When I contemplate the meaning of this introversion, I have learned the saying, "It's hurt people that hurt people." So if you can master those feelings for yourself, you can suddenly start to support others.

I want to stress that this journey of self-discovery is life-long. There is no end, so here's the deal: you have to keep working at it until your last breath. Your final lesson is when they shut the lid on the box. But in all seriousness, I think it's about committing to a willingness to work on yourself always. It's not enough to say, "I did this ten years ago," and "I don't need to do it again/anymore as I have already done it," – it's about having a mindset of constantly learning. I'm a firm believer that if we look at the world around us, it's constantly changing. If I learned something ten years ago, then that lesson applied ten years ago! But if I am constantly learning, then I'm up to date. I'm up to speed on what's happening because we also evolve and become different people. The previously learned lessons deepen our understanding but there is now a new dimension because we have new tools and perspectives, so we look at people and situations differently.

I am a stunt performer and an actor and completed a movie called *Courage* in 2022, which will be out in 2023. It's a comedy and was lots of fun. So courage is critical to me. Dr David Hawkins spent 20-plus years working and writing *The Map of Consciousness*. His work is based on a scale of human emotion from 1 to 1,000, from Shame to Enlightenment. Within his scale, courage is at the 200 level, the first step to transformation.

As a stunt performer, it's easy to relate to courage. Everything you do takes courage, but you soon learn to trust that courage will always be there for you. Courage is also necessary on your journey because you must change your mindset from thinking "I can't do that," to telling yourself you can. Sometimes you even believe you are invincible, especially when you have done all the safety checks. Every day is a journey, and courage becomes part of your DNA. You build excellent courage muscle when you practise and establish good healthy habits because you evolve daily.

Furthermore, I know that courage only appears when connected to something important to you. We don't get courageous or get fearful unless something has meaning. Maybe the first step for me was to realise what was important to me; to discover my values and beliefs. In personal development, I have heard that courage is the beginning of standing up for something you care about.

Having done stunts in movies and other media, everybody thinks I have no fear. But the reality is that I question why my anxiety is often diminished. After pondering this question, I realised we mitigate the risk. I have my team, and the people I surround myself with often see things differently, which helps me prepare and consider all the contingencies; therefore, it's deemed a very safe thing to do. There is, of course, an element of danger, but there's an element of danger walking across the street!

I also think that courage comes from a life change, which is often fearful and scary for you. Many of us are afraid of the dark. So what do we do to eliminate that fear as we turn on the light? We lean into the analogy of everything becoming brighter, more visible, transparent and less frightening. When you consider making a change in your life, one of the biggest things you can do is pause, reflect and think about it. All too often, we rush in. Look at the future, explore the possibilities, try and get help from others, and start bringing these things in little by little until the light appears. In other words, the more clarity around something, the less frightening it becomes.

It's funny when you first realise you have inner courage that allows you to do crazy things and take risks. It just seems to be there one day without thinking. I believe it's the habits we form that we don't notice at the time, but it appears like magic after a while. When I contemplate my courage, a part of me wants to make a joke and call it stupidity. Sometimes the danger is ignored, but there is a grain of truth in that courage fuels us to take action when we're so focused on the mission. We often forget the difficulty, but if you focus on the problem, you'll always see the dilemma. It's a self-fulfilling prophecy notion. You have to focus on what you want. So when I'm doing stunts, for example, we prepare the best we can, and then we don't look at the danger anymore. We look at the outcome that we're trying to create.

The same is internally true for me. There are lots of things that still scare me. I'm not super great at relationships with the opposite sex. But I'm not super great because I'm shy, timid and intimidated by women, especially powerful women. And so, how do I face those kinds of situations with courage? I ignore what the possible outcomes could be, and I do it anyway.

I think sometimes the learning of certain things is found in the activity. Nothing happens with thoughts swimming around in your head; they stay there and remain thoughts. Only when you put your ideas into action does anything happen or change. So we often gain courage with momentum rather than courage in contemplation. This is a big challenge for many as they contemplate a thing until they hope they've figured it out, and then the time has passed. Sometimes in life, you only get a lightning-strike size of a window of opportunity, and if you don't take advantage of it right now, there may never be another opportunity. There's a balance between learning what you can and just jumping in and hoping for the best.

You need to get started, and the momentum within the process will help you. I think there's a significant difference between motivation and impetus because motivation focuses on how we feel. So if you don't feel like doing something, it's hard to motivate yourself to do something when you don't feel like it, but if you get started on it, even if you don't feel like it, it becomes easier. Waking up early in the morning or talking to somebody about an upcoming stunt can be a chore, but if I even get a little bit started, somehow, I can keep going. It's easier to keep it going versus getting motivated to do whatever.

Of course, if you are intrinsically motivated, it will be linked to a more significant 'why', and you will do it automatically rather than relying on external motivation. I think it connects to courage. I love what Mel Robbins has talked about with his five-second rule. Count to five before making your decision. Courage links to your beliefs as sometimes you impulsively jump in, and what, according to the proverb, happens? They say leap, and the net will appear. Take a leap of faith.

I don't see the world as competitive. There's enough space, opportunity, benefits, blessings, abundance, everything to fill in the blank, whatever you want. There's enough for everybody. I feel like we're all so unique in our different ways. Many people don't want the same thing I want, and I don't want what they want, and my set of skills leads me down a different path than their set of skills. I believe there's a grave danger in today's world as we're also competing with everyone's 'shining moments'. For example, what we see on social media isn't the reality. So why compete? Because what people are often showing you is their very best day. Very few take a picture of when they're crying or sitting miserably in the corner and post it on social media. They take their best shot, the best lunch they ever had and the best kitty cat they've ever seen. You can fill in the blanks. Social media is a fantasy that captures a moment that may reflect some aspect of reality but is unsustainable.

The reality is, I think we need to step back and recognise that genuine authenticity isn't about how others feel about you, but it's how you feel about yourself. I try to create moments that I can be proud of and for those I love and care about, whether they're my family or people that are important to me, so that they can feel comfortable about what they see. I don't want to do anything that my mother or other family members would be embarrassed about. I want to do things that ignite me, but not everybody, including my family, gets it. In these situations, it's OK, but I do 'get' it, and I feel great about it.

I often give seminars all over the world, including on cruise ships. During one such forum, I talked about 'Happiness is not a choice'. It is more about changing your perspective to realise that happiness creates positives outcomes i.e. you step into abundance. I'm always trying to figure out what results I can create for my biography. When I die, and somebody writes my biography, will there be a chapter that I would consider embarrassing, or am I going to want the whole picture of me there? Therefore, I need to live my life to reflect my desire to be the best version of myself. However, I am human, and I don't get it right every time, and I don't think anybody is perfect. But when you're aware of it, you can make it better than if you randomly allow things to happen to you.

My authenticity underpins my values. The word 'authenticity' has a lot in common with the word 'author' and 'authorises'. When something in our life requires us to be authentic, we make those decisions ahead of time. We decide who we want to be, and then we authorise those activities as they appear, or we do not authorise them and set up boundaries. We are the author of everything that we do. However, it isn't easy to be authentic if you haven't thought about the kind of life you want to create. You start following what everybody else says you should do, which is the beginning of giving away your power. The more you give away that power, the less you will have. And we start living according to... what your family wants, what your employer wants, what your culture wants, what your society wants, anything rather than what you want.

I'm not saying that doing something that someone else wants for you is always wrong because I think there can be some awesome things that your family can encourage you to do, to bring out the best in you. But how much of yourself are you losing in that process? If we decide who we want to be ahead of time, we can achieve that with passion and purpose. Now you can understand all or some of the values that underpin who you are in life.

I once talked with speaker and transformational coach John Demartini about this idea related to the word passion. He pointed out that the original meaning of passion isn't the exciting feeling we've now come to know it as; it is a willingness to sacrifice, such as the passion of Christ. What do you love so much that you're willing to give up other things for it? For example, you may love the cinema but something else has a higher calling, a passion. The caveat, however, is that there is always an element of sacrifice, because you can't do everything. However, if you change your mindset, you will understand that it is not a sacrifice, because you're choosing the best; that's my philosophy on life.

Making choices is a significant aspect of life; choosing what is good and plentiful. And how do we choose good things? How do we find extraordinary? I've settled for 'good' things too often, whereas now I snatch the potential for 'extraordinary'.

The first valuable lesson of strength I have learned about myself is not to believe you're crap. Sometimes the best lesson on strength is a bit outside of your comfort zone, but be open to your critics, especially those who care about you and are not good communicators. They can say hard truths, often things you need to hear. It's a complex notion to be strong and feel those things that are hard to think of because it is invariably the truth; that's my number one lesson. The second is being willing to learn and allow. Ask yourself if you are still willing to allow yourself to do so. Do you strive for more significance? Be very careful that you don't become stagnant.

I recognise that it's a strength to keep going, too, because I often think that once we reach a specific goal, it becomes straightforward to take a break. That is the last thing you should do because you are back to this idea of building momentum. You lose that momentum when you take a break, and the next thing you want to do can flounder. Now you are back at the beginning, and you have to restart and get up to speed before you can do the next project.

My philosophy is never to slow down. Be careful, though, because the most significant danger of not slowing down is finding the balance in the process. It's like spinning many plates at one time. I firmly believe that when people make a to-do list, it is often way too long. I've some friends who put 20 things on their to-do lists. Instead, I have a long-term goal where I set various targets in my life and within the long-term goals; you only do one or two daily things.

When I interviewed Jack Canfield for my 2008 movie, *The Opus*, he talked about writing *Chicken Soup for the Soul*, one of the top bestselling personal development books. He shared that he and his co-author, Mark Victor Hansen, would pick five things to do every day. Once those five things were done, be it talking to a PR company, giving an interview or signings at a bookstore, then they would feel good that they had accomplished their goals for the day. Sometimes, people bite off more than they can chew, making them frustrated because things don't happen immediately. You cannot do 50 things daily unless you want to experience being overwhelmed. When people try to do too much, they often end up doing nothing instead because it's too intimidating.

I pick several items for my list, which I call 'absolutes'. The others are nice to have but not always necessary to complete in one day, so I might have ten things on my list, but once I get my absolutes done and I feel like I can keep going, I will.

I think it also helps to learn to reward yourself. The best thing I do on my list is a delegate – I find somebody else who can do it, sometimes even better than I can! I'll instruct them what to do and ask that they report back. I am fortunate to have intelligent people around me whom I hire to do my best work, as they know what to do. They know and understand the goal, and they'll report back when they've got a certain amount of whatever completed, and then they are ready for the next step. I mainly use this strategy when I am on holiday or giving seminars on a cruise ship. I've got people working for me; you have to learn to delegate to live your best life because your best life attracts everything to you.

In addition to delegating, it is also about learning to trust the right people. I believe that not everybody has the same capabilities, desires or interests in specific tasks. If you're managing a business or making a movie, how do you find the right person for that right job? The other thing I think is interesting is that I work with many entrepreneurs and coach them on what we have discussed here. The reality is many entrepreneurs try to do all the jobs themselves. In their defence, they tell me it's because no one can do it as well as them. My response is, "Are you doing everything perfectly anyway?" And they tell me no. I come back with, "Well then, why wouldn't you delegate it to someone else if you're doing the task at 70%?" That person may also do it at 70%, but they could do it even better. The bottom line is you're still going to make a lot of money, and no one is perfect. So don't wait for the ideal employee or think you're the perfect employee. You're simply muddling up your system; if you're a cog in the wheel, you're a cog in the rotation, so get out of the way.

Tips to my younger self would include: worry less and have more fun. When we're younger, we're very preoccupied with what the future will bring, and we get worried about it and often self-sabotage ourselves. We hold ourselves back. We are afraid to try new things and do things. I now ride my motorbike a heck of a lot faster. I do more crazy things that probably are harmful. I do more of everything. I take on more life because I think we learn some things over time, and I'm not just talking about dangerous things; I'm talking about anything in life. I think sometimes we play cautious, right? We don't love enough. We don't give enough. We don't care enough. We don't…

I would advise being kinder to myself and others. We would have more capacity for kindness if we centred ourselves and refrained from belittling or criticising ourselves. We often don't believe we're capable of the things we can do; therefore, we limit ourselves. You can do anything you put your mind to, so start doing it.

The final thing I'd advise is to take as many people with you because I don't think we do that often enough when we do exciting stuff. We're so concerned about ourselves in the process. In my experience, I have found that if you lift others and bring others with you, success and abundance follow. Success is a team sport, so quit trying to do everything yourself.

Meeting Dexter Moscow is a gift from God; you know, one of those special people who cross your path in life. In the chapter you are about to read, you will be inspired, uplifted and humbled by the sincerity of this Voice of Strength.

Dexter knows the power of vulnerability, and when you read his story, you will soon understand the depth of his beautiful soul. His life experiences are clearly explained and will undoubtedly be food for thought for you.

Dexter believes in lifelong learning, evident in all he has read, undertaken and shared in his life and business. The focus on positive psychology, and all of the other variants and gurus, exemplifies the determination to deepen his understanding of the trauma faced at a young age, and release him from its grip.

I am sure that many of the insights shared will inspire you to reflect on what trauma and pain you continue to hold on to. Some of his practices might just be what you need.

Brenda

Dexter Moscow

"The only thing we have control over is our reaction to any given situation."

Dexter Moscow

The Power of Vulnerability

"Vulnerability is not weakness;
it's our greatest measure of courage."

Brené Brown,
author and research professor,
University of Houston.

I hope that by declaring my vulnerability, told through the stories drawn from the pages of my book *A Voyage Without My Father*, it will offer guidance, and direction, and give you the strength to realise your full potential, to show your vulnerability and tell **your** story.

To stand apart from the crowd, dare to be different and close your ears to the naysayers around you, so that you can follow your dream.

A Life Cut Short: Life Lessons Learnt

At the age of ten, I suffered the devastating loss of my father, who was only 45 when he died. This obviously affected me as I grew up, but I believe the full impact of his passing came much later in my life. The feelings of anger, sadness, regret and loneliness resurfaced at significant times of life-cycle events and became even more intense when I became a husband, father and grandfather.

When my father passed, and for reasons that I still cannot fully comprehend, I was not allowed to visit him in hospital and ultimately was not there to say goodbye and tell him I loved him before he died.

This has been, and remains to this day, a deep regret that has coloured my attitude to life, and my reactions to life events and to relationships, both personal and business.

All this emotional baggage came to a head when I was in my mid-thirties and culminated in two pivotal moments that led me on a journey of self-discovery that I relate here.

The first such moment happened when I was driving to my estate agent's office in Wealdstone, Middlesex.

I was merrily singing along to a song on the radio when the next track was announced: Mike and the Mechanics, *The Living Years*. The song contains a specific lyric that is the embodiment of my sadness at the loss of my dad: "I wasn't there that morning when my father passed away."

Even today, the song brings a lump to my throat and on that fateful morning the tears started welling in my eyes to such an extent that it blurred my vision and I had to pull over to the side of the road. I found myself sobbing uncontrollably and realised that after 25 years, this was a reaction that had to be explored.

The second and more profound experience was when my twin boys were approaching their tenth birthday.

I found myself becoming more and more short-tempered and getting unreasonably angry at seemingly unimportant things. I never chastised my boys physically. I was a shouter and my voice would strike fear into them. This was unacceptable, I realised, as it was affecting my precious relationship with my sons, a relationship which, for obvious reasons, I never had with my own father.

It came to a head on Christmas morning.

I had asked them to stand in front of the Christmas tree to pose in their C-3PO golden costumes which has been left by Father Christmas to be discovered that very morning. (For those of you who don't know, C-3PO is the much-loved robotic character from the *Star Wars* films!)

As kids do, they were mucking around, much preferring to play with their lightsabers than stand for a photo. So, I shouted.

The reaction was immediate and to this very day brings a feeling of guilt. They stood stock-still, their bottom lips trembling and trying to hold back the tears.

What should have been a joyous morning full of fun and laughter, had instead been turned into a traumatic experience for them and me. After discussing it with my wife Fran, she suggested I go and see Dr Friedman, an eminent psychiatrist, whom she had been seeing to resolve her fear of descending escalators.

Dr Friedman was a dour, unemotional man – a practised demeanour, I'm sure – who sat there with tented fingers, asking me questions and nodding sagely. He offered and recommended pathways that would lead me to recognise why I reacted in certain ways to my children and the world in general. He gave me methodologies and processes to deal with my anger. These 'talking therapies' are of course very effective for a lot of people and on reflection, I'm sure helped me through day-to-day problems.

We met once a month for a period of 18 months at his Harley Street practice, and during these sessions we discussed many things. Parenting, marital challenges, filial relationships, and life in general. Many of these conversations are long forgotten but it was through these sessions that Dr Friedman helped me identify the root cause of my short-temperedness with my sons and others. It would rear its ugly head specifically when the boys cried over some seemingly inconsequential situation.

With the benefit of hindsight, it seems blatantly obvious what was going on.

Hidden deep in my psyche, the following conversation was taking place: "When I was ten my father died, so why should you be upset about something as trivial as a lost toy or not liking the food placed before you?"

What then? My anger was directed at my boys and at life in general, because I could not be angry at my father. He was dead and how can you blame someone for dying? The understanding this gave me certainly helped me become less angry. If I found the ire rising, then I could rationalise the feeling and prevent it from spilling over to disrupt my life, but I couldn't confront him and vent my anger.

The fact that he was overweight, a chain smoker and generally unfit, certainly were contributory factors to his heart condition, but ANGRY AT MY FATHER FOR DYING??

OK, what do I do with that? I couldn't tell him how much his loss had impacted my life. How his absence at so many important life events had cast a dark shadow over those moments.

That he would never meet his grandchildren, my wife, see me develop as a man, and would not be there to teach me how to be a good father. Or could I?

In the late eighties, I discovered – or should I say it found me? – The Silva Mind Control Method, now known as The Silva Method, a programme that enables us to control how we think and respond to situations rather than, as the title suggests, controlling other people's minds. In its purest form, The Silva Method is a self-help and meditation programme developed by José Silva who was an American self-taught parapsychologist and author.

It claims to increase an individual's abilities to develop higher brain functions, increase brain power and over time, gain psychic abilities, all through relaxation.

Fran and I sought out this programme in the hope that it would help our identical twin boys gain processes and tools to aid them with their A-level studies, giving them the skills to increase their recall abilities and reduce their exam anxiety.

The Silva Method was the first Mind Expanding Technique we experienced and is a mixture of self-hypnosis and meditation, including some elements from Neuro Linguistic Programming, about how Neuro Linguistic Programming can overcome very quickly phobias.

In essence, these concepts, which I later discovered are akin to Gestalt Therapy, offered a complete set of tools needed to control our minds.

So how did these tools help me resolve the deep-seated anger at my father? Using this very pragmatic meditative process, I closed my eyes and using the method we had been taught, I counted myself down from ten to one, to reach the Alpha level.

In my mind, I stood outside the hospital ward where, as a child, I had been forbidden to enter. I pushed open one of the double doors and walked towards the bed that I imagined my father had occupied.

I visualised him sitting up and noticed the pained expression on his face. I smelt that all-pervading odour that all hospitals seem to have and noticed the green of the curtains dividing patient from patient and the light coming from atop his bed.

What then? My meditation training had taught me these tricks of engaging all of the senses to make the experience as real as possible.

Physically, I felt weighed down, my throat was dry and my heart was beating fast. It was not as in a dream, where we feel swept along by the situation; here I was in control, certain of my surroundings, perhaps less so of my emotions.

In my head I heard my trembling voice, "Dad, why did you leave me when I needed you so much? You weren't there for my confirmation, my wedding, or my children. I've missed you and still do." I related the situations where his absence had scarred me.

I don't remember what was actually said either by me or him. I know we both cried, I sobbed, and we hugged. There was an actual physical sensation. It is amazing what the mind can create!

I counted myself out from this deep meditative state, 5-4-3-2-1, stating the following affirmation as I opened my eyes: "As I count myself up from five to one, I will open my eyes feeling wide awake, happy, healthy and confident in my abilities in the certain knowledge that something miraculous would happen in my life."

Coming back to the real world, I felt calm and as if a weight had been lifted from my heart. The anger dissipated and only a deep love remained. Regularly the conversations continue and whenever I feel troubled or confused, I return to speak to my dad knowing that he is watching over me and will always be at my side.

This may appear to be a mind trick and in fact, it is. It is the same mind trick that prayer can induce, that is spoken about in every religious or other discipline that acknowledges something greater than us, whether that is a deity or a collective consciousness.

The Bible talks of God's 'still small voice', or is it the voice within us, that when we are quiet and contemplative, comes to us as in a whisper to direct us?

Whatever you choose to believe, whatever serves to take you from a negative state to a more constructive frame of mind, seek out what works for you and use it.

Was it courageous to change my mindset? I believe it was more a realisation that living a life full of regret was damaging to my well-being and those around me.

Since these early days, I have found other supportive processes to strengthen my belief that I can be whatever I choose to be and not "a hostage to others' hopes and fears" to paraphrase the lyrics from *The Living Years*.

One such discipline is Stoicism, a philosophy that flourished for some 400 years in Ancient Greece and Rome. It had one overwhelming and highly practical ambition: to teach people how to be calm and brave in the face of overwhelming anxiety and pain.

At the root of Stoicism is the understanding that *"The only thing we have control over is our reaction to any given situation."* It's my mantra and affirmation for life.

A further aspect of being a Stoic is *"Stoicism is focusing on things that are in your control, getting rid of negative emotions and finding opportunity in every obstacle."* Phil Van Treuren, writer, artist, entrepreneur.

Another process that gives me the strength to suffer *"The slings and arrows of outrageous fortune,"* to quote Shakespeare's *Hamlet*, is Positive Intelligence.

Developed by Shirzad Chamine, a Harvard University Professor, it is a daily visualisation process that recognises that there are negative voices in our head that tell us we are not worthy, we will fail, or we are not clever enough.

By recognising our success and that these voices are telling us lies, we can turn down the volume on them and change our perception to a more life-enhancing view. What once was told to us by our parents, teachers and others does not necessarily hold true today.

"Don't talk to strangers", "Speak only when you are spoken to", "Don't interrupt", "The harder you work, the more success your gain."

And the greatest lie of all…

"Work Hard & You'll Succeed." It should, of course, be "Work smarter."

ooo

Recently I have discovered the teaching of Deepak Chopra, who through a free 21-day guided mediation programme has changed my belief about abundance.

Warren Buffett, the American business magnate, investor, and philanthropist, said that the most important investment he made in himself was to attend a Dale Carnegie presentation skills course and I'm proud to say that I am a trained Dale Carnegie Trainer.

The second investment Warren makes in himself is to meditate. Every morning, before he opens his computer or looks at his phone, he takes time out to be quiet.

If it's good enough for one of the world's richest men, it's good enough for me!

In a world where, through the media, we are constantly fed messages of lack and shortage, it is refreshing to hear another viewpoint.

"Today I behold all the abundance that surrounds me."
Deepak Copra

When we lead our lives authentically, with gratitude, love, integrity and with the intention of helping our fellow human beings, we will reap the rewards we deserve.

These life lessons and coping strategies I have illustrated can be summed up in the following sentences:

- Be kind to yourself.

- Take time out of your working day to reflect on what you have achieved, whether big or small.

- Count your blessings.

- Draw those you love closer to you.

It has taken most of my life to realise that I am stronger than I have ever thought possible, and I am worthy of all that life has to give.

Would I have done things differently? Some things, of course. What advice would I give to my younger self?

- Enjoy every moment. You don't know when the end will come.

- Seek the advice of others and value their experience.

- Look for mentors or let them find you.

- Everything happens for a reason, find the gift in every situation.

- Perfection is for the gods, not for us mere mortals.

- We learn more from our so-called failures than our successes.

Napoleon Hill, author of *Think and Grow Rich*, said, *"Most great people have attained their greatest success one step beyond their greatest failure."*

And although I'm sure this story below is apocryphal, it is still a great story of personal power.

One night, President Obama and his wife Michelle decided to do something out of the ordinary and have a casual dinner at a restaurant that wasn't too luxurious. Once they were seated, the owner of the restaurant asked the President's Secret Service chief if he could please speak to the First Lady in private.

The chief obliged, and Michelle had a conversation with the owner. When she returned to the table, President Obama asked Michelle why the owner was so interested in speaking with her. She told her husband that, when they were teenagers, he had been madly in love with her.

"So if you had married him," President Obama said, "you would now be the owner of this lovely restaurant?"

"No," Michelle replied. "If I had married him, he would now be the President!"

TO YOUR SUCCESS AND INCREASING POWER.

Dexter Moscow – The Picasso of Sales Presentations, Author, Professional Speaker

You often hear the phrase "Be brave". Shareef Amin, a British veteran, embodies courage and bravery. I met Shareef in the capacity of a publisher, and I felt humbled by his choice to share his story with me.

In this chapter, you will find a Voice of Strength that puts the lives of others in Ukraine before his safety. Some may consider that foolish, but when you live purposefully, saying yes to a cause greater than yourself becomes easy. You will begin to understand the humanitarian behind the man and what drives him to give his life for the sake of those who cannot defend themselves.

You may be curious about what it takes to join the army and fight in wars, so reading Shareef's account will lead you to his strong belief in working on yourself, especially your mindset. What makes us human is that we have free will to make choices, some good and some bad. Learning from those not-so-good choices will determine your path in life.

Shareef continues to walk in his light despite the plight he now faces. He knows the true power of learning life lessons and using them to improve the quality of your choices.

Brenda

Shareef Amin

"Courage, for me, is my instinct; I have an idea and go for it. I do not fear where I go or the outcome."

Shareef Amin

I have always forged my own path. Sometimes the main road was blocked by racism, childhood bullying and being pushed aside by adults who should have known better – i.e. teachers. School was challenging as I have dyslexia and dyspraxia, although nobody seemed to take any notice of my learning difficulties.

As I grew into a teenager, I began to be me. I did not look like the other kids. I preferred a Mohican-style haircut and wore tight trousers tucked into my socks. I dare say some called me a misfit, so I behaved in a way that fulfilled other people's assumptions. Like many young people who do not fit in but are born to stand out, I fell into a 'wrong' crowd as my years at secondary school came to a close. I was more out of school than in, so gaining qualifications was not my priority. I was lost, but I did not fully understand this at the time.

I come from a multicultural family, an Iraqi father and a British mother with strong religious beliefs, which fuelled my quest to find my identity. Growing up, my relationship with my father was everything, and I loved to spend time with him. He is my hero, and his solid work ethic, determination and love of people have rubbed off on me. As they say, the apple does not fall far from the tree.

My father always looked out for me, and so continuing that strong bond we had developed throughout my childhood,

I worked with him in his video shop when I left school. He also provided me with the flat above the shop so I could learn to stand on my own two feet and take some responsibility for my life. At every turn, it seemed I was different to the other young men my age. I took it in my stride and thought nothing of it because I was still standing out, not always for the right reasons, but life throws us challenges to shape us into good human beings.

As a young boy, I was fascinated with war, not from the physical fighting perspective, but from the notion of fighting for freedom. I have this strong sense of injustice: I must defend those wronged, oppressed and suppressed.

After 9/11, a pathway cleared in front of me. My obsession with the Armed Forces and the terror raging in the USA ignited the idea of following my passion. It was a toss-up of joining either the police or the Army. Given my lack of qualifications, I decided that the Army was the route for me, so I joined the infantry. The training was tough and took me longer than expected; another obstacle I had to face, accept and overcome. But with steely determination, I carried on. I was making a huge decision that would impact my life, and it felt good. I was doing something that would benefit me and the world.

After training, I was posted to Afghanistan twice, where I could use my training to keep people safe, defend their villages and towns, and do what I could to make a difference. That was at the heart of what I did, and I knew I had to use my life to make a difference.

Following the Army, I returned to Civvy Street, which was challenging. In the Army, I wore a uniform, was part of a team and had a clear identity. As a single man, I did not receive help like my counterparts who were married with children. I drifted for a time, drinking, gambling and taking drugs. Having been a fine specimen of a man physically in the Army, I soon craved having that better version of Shareef. So I cleaned myself up, hit the gym and took a course on Protection and Security; after all, this was where my skills lay.

No sooner had I got myself organised on another path, than on 24th February 2022 I watched the news that Ukraine was being invaded by Russia. Once again, a sense of injustice rose within me. Now I had the skills to protect and defend. It only took the Ukraine President, Volodymyr Zelenskyy, to request support from the world, that I knew what would be my next step. Somehow I knew I had to go and support the Ukrainians. I am a man taking responsibility for making a difference, and my humanitarian heart forged yet another path that lay before me.

Unfortunately, I was injured in action in Ukraine, and am now recuperating. I believe I am an example of what is possible when you make your mind up to take action and make a difference in the world because you CAN.

I have a deep sense of courage forged by the experiences and situations I have found myself in throughout my life. At first, you don't recognise your courage because it is a part of you. Courage, for me, is my instinct; I have an idea and I go for it. I do not fear where I go or the outcome. Courage is forging your path and enjoying the experiences along the way. When you develop this attitude, the belief in yourself strengthens, so you keep going and never entertain the idea of giving up. You have to be honest, though, because there are some failures along the route, but you get back up again and carry on. Problem solving becomes a part of the mission, and I find that exhilarating.

A positive mindset is crucial to your success at whatever you attempt. I am not saying that it is easy, but you build a toolkit so that when you fall, fear or fade, you can choose what to do to restore your energy and the will to continue. Taking time out to recharge your batteries is essential when you work extremely hard. I did this while in Ukraine. Sometimes war is too much, and you have to get away. So I would go to Odessa, a beautiful city, to revitalise my energy and enjoy rest and relaxation beside the sea before regrouping for the next mission. You must let your hair down and do what makes you feel alive and good. Then it is easy to keep going. However, do not mix up taking an intended break, from letting your goal fizzle out. It is entirely different. An intended break takes a strong mind, whereas allowing something to fizzle out takes a mind that is not connected to the goal.

When you have a strong mindset and a positive outlook, your actions will always follow this way of thinking. I always focus on the feeling I want to enjoy and take the appropriate steps to get those feelings. My actions drive my aspiration to serve others and make a difference; that is why I keep going and look for opportunities to do just that. When I am helping, others give meaning to my life. It makes me feel good, and I want more of that. I have been on the dark side, which is not a place I want to frequent, for those feelings do not make you or anyone feel good. I choose happiness, so I do what brings that to me in bucket loads. You can too.

I sometimes question and ponder what being a man who lives authentically in a competitive world really is. I think society is changing, and we are more open to looking at men and women in a different light. I call myself a humanitarian because people are at the core of who I am; my purpose, passion and mission. Therefore, I often contemplate what it means to be a human. When you think about being human, it dissolves the differences many men put in the way. They are old school, and as we can see, there are still too many patriarchal societies around the world. Again, this raises my strong sense of injustice.

Men are beginning to be more open and talk about their feelings. Putting mental health in the ring of conversations has played a vital role in opening the door to the opportunity to speak out. The internet, television and mental health charities provide us with lots of information, platforms and opportunities to find other people like ourselves. When you face your truth, you connect with being authentic, which I say is being true to yourself. You can bullshit others, but you can never bullshit yourself. When you do, you feel 'off' and become angry, resentful and jealous. Thank God we are now being encouraged to shed tears when we feel like it, instead of the old school ideas such as that it's weak for men to cry, pull yourself together, and so on.

Perhaps being neurodiverse has something to do with me being authentic? Having a great role model in my dad, who demonstrated being authentic by caring for his family and doing whatever it took to put food on the table, laid the solid foundations we all need to thrive. I have values and live by these, along with my principles, which then became my moral compass, enabling me to make good decisions that benefit me into being a better version of myself. However, you need to be careful and not completely ignore the opinions of others. If they are opinions from a trusted source, you should consider them before making up your mind.

My decision to join the Army was welcomed and encouraged by my dad, but when I decided to go to Ukraine, I faced some resistance. I suppose it was because I was not attached to the Army but going alone with a group of others who felt the same way as I did. However, my drive was so strong that eventually, my family knew that I would go with or without their blessing, so they gave it to me because they loved me. Perhaps I was being selfish, but I was on a mission to make a difference in the lives of people who did not know how to. I did; the British Army had trained me.

When it comes to competition, I think men are naturally competitive. Being in the Army showed me that competition was fierce. But if you connect to who you are on the inside, you begin to ignore the outer competition and focus on making yourself better each day; then, you naturally improve and beat others anyway. That is my experience, and I will always do things to the best of my ability. In my world, where you are keeping people safe, you want to teach them the best of what you know so they can defend themselves, others and their villages.

There is a time and place for competition, such as in games and sport, but competing in life is a dangerous game, and it robs you of enjoying the process where all the learning takes place. So focus on yourself and beat your own competition, and you will feel great. Learn to use and trust your intuition, for it is rarely wrong.

One of the valuable lessons I have learnt about myself is that I am my best student. Men don't often speak about inner strength, and it's more likely to be about building physical strength by going to the gym, lifting weights, and working on your muscles and six-pack.

Inner strength is about your resilience. When you work muscles correctly, they get stronger. When you encounter knock-backs, see going to the gym as an opportunity to build and strengthen your resilience. Ask yourself how you bounce back when you experience a setback. Do you crumble, go into overdrive, or bury your head in the sand? Find ways to deal with it in a proactive way where you are taking control.

Do not let experiences and situations get you down; instead, see them as challenges, even battles you can win. Look to other people who have gone through similar experiences and read their stories. How did they overcome their situations and challenges? Find the common threads and tools.

As a man who left school with few qualifications, sometimes life teaches you that you need to find the lessons in all things, to find the ways you like to learn. Read, talk to others, research, write, and watch YouTube videos, TEDx talks or TV programmes that interest you and can offer advice. There is a plethora of material and information available in the world today. Knowledge is king, but applying it opens a new world where you are the king.

We are fortunate to have the internet and social media where you can find like-minded people. That's how I found the group of ex-soldiers that I went to Ukraine with. Be willing to do whatever it takes; that's what is essential, not the outcome. Be prepared to come up against brick walls, not find the answers straight away, or find yourself going down another road. Know it is part of the journey, and it is the journey, not the destination, that teaches you, so you might as well enjoy it!

When you choose to keep going, resilience strengthens. When you pick yourself up, dust yourself down and start all over again, as the song goes, you can begin to understand what it is to be resilient. I believe the Army taught me that, too, because you cannot let your squad down as a team and must learn to keep going by picking yourself up. Of course, the camaraderie helps as you are part of a band of brothers who understand what you are going through as a soldier. So you have to find your band of brothers or tribe that you can rely on to keep you going during the tough times. It is always about strengthening your resilience.

There are three tips I would tell the younger Shareef.

1. I would tell him to create a good habit around physical fitness and improving strength, and stick with it. As your body grows and becomes stronger, your mind becomes stronger, and you become more confident.

2. To understand that everyone else is not you, so do not put expectations on them. When you expect something from someone and they do not deliver, it is easy to become upset, hurt or broken. Not everyone lives by your standards, and sometimes it is challenging to understand why they do not behave like you. All that matters is that YOU are a good person. The reciprocation from others does not mean they are bad, but simply that they do not reflect who you are in life. Your job is to rise above these behaviours and be you.

3. To set short-term goals and aim high. It may take you a while to achieve your dream, but by setting small goals towards your big one, you will always go beyond your first thought.

I learned these lessons later in life. It is vital for your happiness and mental health to do these things now rather than waiting for a better tomorrow, and create the life you want by making better choices.

"It is worth remembering that the time of greatest gain in terms of wisdom and inner strength is often that of greatest difficulty."

Dalai Lama

"It's not where you start but where you finish" are the words of a song from the 1970's Broadway hit, *Seesaw*. Dennis Pitocco illustrates that you cannot blame your life choices on your humble beginnings. His strong work ethic enabled him to rise through the career ranks before deciding to forge a new path with his wife, Ali. Dennis has found his true purpose in life, which directs his focus on humanity and how he can use his gifts and talents to make it better each day.

Gratitude and awareness of his blessings led him to focus on giving back through a range of activities before developing his company, 360° Nation. Dennis found his purpose of giving back through a global community. His story reveals the power of dreaming, setting goals and visualising that they will come true one day. It is not your business to know when or how. A deep-rooted trust stirs within and gives you a Voice of Strength to live by your convictions.

Dennis hints at a story of conscious selflessness and behaviour steeped in making yourself the best version so that our world is a better place; one person, one voice, one day at a time, so you can live life as the real YOU.

Brenda

Dennis Pitocco

"If we are serious in our quest to rediscover humanity at its best, then our job is to walk the talk today and every day, doing our best to figure out what the world is trying to be – and then help the world be that, be better, and be even more."

Dennis Pitocco

Looking Back

I grew up in Pittsburgh, PA, as one of eight children, in a large happy Italian family, but with no prospects to attend college due to family economics. I enlisted in the Air Force at the age of 17, leaving home soon after my high school graduation. Hawaii was home for the duration of my military service.

Following my military service, I moved into a banking career (via a USAF job placement service) and spent 30+ years rising through the ranks. I left banking to start a financial services business with a good friend, and never looked back, as we ultimately found success across the USA, Canada and the UK. I met my wife Ali in the UK and together, we decided to sell all of our business interests and settle down in Tampa Bay to begin the next chapter of our life together.

This chapter was defined over the course of our ongoing morning walks, away from all the noise. We ultimately decided to devote our time, our talent and our treasure towards giving back. This led to hands-on involvement with non-profit organisations (locally, nationally and internationally), from grassroots level to boardroom level. And it ultimately led to the creation of 360° Nation, our global media enterprise, and GoodWorks 360°, our pro-bono, non-profit consulting foundation. Blessed with ample financial success from our past business careers, we pivoted to doing what made "sense versus cents" as, together, we began our lifetime endeavour to rediscover humanity at its best.

Looking Forward

As we launched 360° Nation, we had to 'unlearn' the need for a precise business plan, allowing our global audience to shape the direction of our business over time. Along the way, we've reacted, reinvented, refocused and repositioned all that we do to best serve our global community. Essentially, we've continued to break the status quo to make it better.

We've said for a long time that our job is to figure out what the world is trying to be – and then help the world be that, be better and be even more. The world depends on every single one of us showing up, being present, and as best we can, individually and collectively creating positive ripples of change – one person, one voice, one step at a time. Without question, a healthy mix of courage, passion and strength of conviction has continued to be the 'wind beneath our wings'. Much of that courage has come from the amazing support of our rapidly expanding, worldwide conscious community. As our business continues to expand, we continue to reflect upon and embrace the storied quote from Margaret Sheppard.

"Sometimes, the only available transportation is a leap of faith."

Pivoting To Do More Good

The COVID pandemic forced us to step back and reposition our approach to rediscovering humanity, ultimately triggering the launch of 360° Nation Studios and a number of other virtual/production channels focused on elevating voices across the universe 'for good'. The silver lining beneath it all was a reinvigorating purpose, along with a greater opportunity to deliver our for good promise. And with that came increasing awareness of the value of each of us discovering and revealing our often vulnerable voices, and sharing those voices with vulnerability and authenticity. Very often, we've heard from our audience that reading someone else's story brought considerable comfort, as they've seen themselves in a similar version of the same story, and now recognise that they are not alone.

Life Reimagined and Wisdom Gained

My life today is not far from that which I envisioned in my twenties in many respects, borne of an entrepreneurial spirit coupled with a willingness to be a risk-taker from day one of my career. My perspectives have been formed over the course of a substantial amount of international travel over the years, allowing me an opportunity to watch the evening news through a more informed lens. It's all about being a part of something bigger than ourselves, embracing the magic of authentic community, thriving with people who share different interests, bound together with a common goal; to rediscover humanity at its very best.

I have zero regrets, and consequently have never imagined going back to an earlier stage of life, but rather focus all of my thoughts on (re)imagining and crafting my particular corner of the future. Looking back, the most valuable lesson learned, without exception, has been to continually define myself by doing the right thing, even when no one is watching. That includes walking my talk when it comes to the many values we both espouse across all of our for good activities.

It has been the unexpected and extraordinary strength, borne of community and genuine connection, that has allowed me to spread my entrepreneurial wings far and wide, discovering infinite possibilities while engendering amazing, genuine relationships along the way.

Everything Works Better When You Unplug It for a While

These days, it seems almost like a foreign concept to be unplugged even for 24 hours. Texts, emails and phone calls that aren't immediately returned are interpreted as being ignored. But what are the implications of that constant feeling of connectedness that binds many of us for as much as 16 to 18 hours per day? Perhaps it requires unplugging to take a true assessment of how far-reaching this technology has become in dictating our lives. We increasingly miss out on the important moments of our lives as we pass the hours with our noses buried in our devices.

As the depth and breadth of our enterprise consumed more and more of our time over the years, we approached the end of our first decade with a mix of excitement and wonder, underpinned by a desire to recognise this pivotal anniversary in a constructively disruptive way – that is a way that would not simply benefit us, but perhaps those who continued to follow our journey.

After considerable thought, we decided to do the unthinkable, particularly as it relates to what had, by design, become a 24/7 operation. We decided to simply unplug!

Unplug? Are you kidding? Far too many write about it, think about it, talk about it, and understand the need for and value of it. But few actually do it with conviction, even if for a few hours, let alone a day, a weekend, a week, or more. Face it – we're all addicted to our devices. Full stop.

OED Definition:

ən'pləg verb: **unplug**; 3rd person present: **unplugs**; past tense: **unplugged**; past participle: **unplugged**; gerund or present participle: **unplugging**

1. disconnect (an electrical device) by removing its plug from a socket.
   "she unplugged the fridge"

   sever the connection between a peripheral device and a computer.
   "the only thing you can do is to unplug the RJ45"

2. remove an obstacle or blockage from.
   "a procedure to unplug blocked arteries"

3. informal

   relax by disengaging from normal activities.
   "they've gone up to the cabin to unplug"

Disconnecting To Reconnect –
Our Radical Sabbatical

We decided it was time for us to walk the talk. That is, to actually step back, exhale, and smell the roses. It was time to bring real meaning to the notion of self-care. It was time for our entire 360° Nation team to disconnect so that we could reconnect with each other and what's really important. We were further inspired to 'just do it' as we stumbled upon this brief story from a publication called *Our Daily Bread.*

> *In 1952, in an effort to prevent clumsy or careless people from breaking items in a shop, a Miami Beach store owner posted a sign that read: "You break it, you buy it." The catchy phrase served as a warning to shoppers. This type of sign can now be seen in many boutiques. However, a different sign was placed in a local potter's shop that read: "If you break it, we'll make it into something better."*

The notion of **"breaking it and making it into something better"** became the framework for what ultimately transpired over the course of our extended break, christened by us as our Radical Sabbatical.

Almost everything works better if you unplug it for a few minutes, including you. **A few minutes? How about a few months?** In our case, **three** glorious months – and boy, are we 'working better' because of it. So many folks across the universe lifted us up with their words of encouragement and support as we set off on our long-planned Radical Sabbatical, that we promised to keep an unplugged journal for sharing upon our return. And we did, in hopes that sharing the highlights of our experience would encourage others; first, to recognise that "self-care isn't selfish" and second, to take a break by totally unplugging from the internet, mobile phone, computer, iPad, and other online devices for a day, two days, a weekend, a week, or even longer. Call it a digital detox, taking as much time as you can to rediscover that elusive 'gift of presence' as we did.

Our Journey of Rediscovery

Looking back, our escape from it all fell into three natural phases that can best be described as **re-discovery**. Unsurprisingly, month one was the decompress and let go month, with us pumping the brakes each day to gradually slow down from 24/7 hustle to 24/7 calm. A month of letting go, transitioning, exhaling, and ultimately surrendering to serenity.

Month two was about (repeatedly) giving ourselves permission to breathe, and simply relax – not seeking to fill every minute of this newfound time with stuff. A lot of reflection and recovery. A recognition that it was much less about our ability and much more about our **availability**. More awareness and authenticity. A state of peaceful bliss, as we cultivated our presence – with less 'doing' and more 'being'. More spontaneity. More fun. We rediscovered the magic of giving important discussions our undivided time and attention versus whatever is left of both at the end of the day.

For us, the feeling of waking up in the morning and just sitting back, becoming more of a participant versus an observer, brought with it an unexpected sense of relief, liberty, and a priceless moment to actually enjoy each moment, just as it is. Again, really listening and talking to each other without distractions just felt a bit like old times, like when we were children.

Noticeable over time was how calm, free, careless and light-hearted we became. Days without interruptions or anxiety. Days of peace and quiet and intentional, wonderful silence. A feeling of timelessness. Surprisingly, the feeling of restless or boredom never entered the picture, as we were so enamoured by a feeling of liberation. We were hooked on the notion of enjoying more with less. Less noise. Less compulsion. Less discomfort. Less reliance. And we developed even more gratitude for the simple ingredients right in front of us for a joyful life.

"Somewhere between handling challenges, taking care of business, and juggling responsibilities, you may have lost pieces of yourself that you long to recover. Perhaps they were buried and forgotten long ago. Rediscovering is more than just being reminded of these golden treasures. It is being able to excavate your riches by pulling them out, polishing them off, and allowing them to shine again."

Susan C. Young
author and motivational speaker

Preserving the Magic

As month three (our final month) came around, we naturally began contemplating our return, but with an escalating determination to fully grasp and preserve the magic of our sabbatical experience along with the priceless wisdom gained. Back on the usual hamster wheel was not for us. We soon recognised that it wasn't really about chasing that elusive work/life **balance,** but rather cultivating the notion of work/life **harmony**. In other words, we needed to step back and reimagine our approach to all that we do to ensure that self-care remained at the forefront and that we didn't simply fall into the Groundhog Day trap – repeating history day after day.

As our final month took us into the new year, our thought process shifted away from the age-old concept of resolutions towards the fresher concept of **dissolutions**; taking things off the table that work against harmony while applying a bit of "if it ain't broke, break it" unconventional wisdom – perhaps making it into something better.

Having escaped all the noise for so long, we were able to move forward with a bit of reckless abandon coupled with an amazing level of clarity and oneness of purpose. Our forward motion was galvanized by an unwavering commitment to approach the reimagination process differently. Question everything. Ditch the unnecessary. Let go. Declutter. Set reasonable versus lofty expectations. Say yes more often without hesitating to say no more often. Nothing sacrosanct. No boundaries. No exceptions. No kidding.

Finding Our Flow

We literally immersed ourselves into what is called a "flow state".

In positive psychology, a flow state (also known colloquially as being in the zone), is the mental state in which a person performing some activity is fully immersed in a feeling of energized focus, full involvement, and enjoyment in the process of the activity. In essence, flow is characterized by the complete absorption in what one does, and a resulting transformation in one's sense of time.

Source: Wikipedia

And that's what we did. And boy, was it transformational across our personal and professional lives!

On the personal front, we immersed ourselves into a series of deep-dive discussions of anything found within our daily life as usual bucket. People. Relationships. Travel. Fun. Not fun. Auto-pilot stuff, etc. Pretty much taking stock of our lives in every respect imaginable. And then we emptied the bucket, sorted out the contents, and determined what was really important and what was not. We refilled the bucket by intentionally shifting our time, attention and focus to the former. A lighter bucket emerged, but one full of more time to discover and enjoy what really matters. An opportunity to bask in the glow of fewer stressors.

We brought the same mindset to everything in our business as usual bucket. Routines. Schedules. To-do lists. Post-it notes. Clutter. Expectations. Pressure points. Angst. Stressors. It was time for business as usual to morph into "business as **unusual**". We literally reimagined everything under our 360° Nation umbrella. Every Page. Every Channel. Every Event. Everything ditched or refreshed. Including a renewed commitment to GoodWorks 360° – our for good foundation.

Looking Back as We Look Forward

In the end, our digital detox evolved into an unplanned, extraordinary journey of self-rediscovery from top to bottom. We developed a keen appreciation for the fact that time is a finite resource; once spent, it's gone. We can't get time back, but we can be selective and purposeful with the time we have and how we spend it. We can take control by 'saying yes to less' and appreciating the white space in our diary. We can protect our precious time for the activities and people that give our lives the most meaning and joy. We rediscovered each other and reaffirmed our purpose, or our 'why'. The 'why' that fuels our passion, encompasses our work, our relationships, that is wrapped around everything we do. We emerged from 'finding our flow', ready to live our lives in a more intentional way, with a sharper focus on everything that really matters.

Take it from us. When we learn to use, enjoy and experience the benefits of technology, but not be attached to it or dominated by it, we are liberated. And with liberation comes that keen awareness of the simple ingredients right in front of us for a joyful life. Our relationships are our bedrock, our foundation. We need to nurture them with the love and attention they really deserve. Though we may be caregivers or breadwinners for others, we need to remember to care for ourselves along the way. Because self-care really truly isn't selfish. Step back for a moment. Take a break. Take some unplugged time every now and then to make the rest of your life the best of your life.

"Go within every day
and find the inner strength
so that the world will not
blow your candle out."
Katherine Dunham

There is something truly magical about a man who faces his truth, especially when he can identify his flaws. It takes courage to do so; it is the first step to transformation. When you connect to that inner voice of truth, you find a strength that allows you to get back onto your feet with new energy, focus and vision. While many people find a rock – a soul mate – the only person we can rely on is ourselves.

Matt Evans woke up one day and realised that he had to think differently, do differently and make better choices, just like many of us.

Inner strength develops through resilience, and Matt speaks about getting back up each day. It's a new start, so embracing it as a catalyst to do better and be better is the focus needed to reveal the true person inside us. In a world that races around, realise that to move further and faster is to slow down. Matt shares the strategies that have enabled him to accept who he is, that he can get back up no matter what, and keep going against all odds.

Reading his chapter will open your eyes to a new way of being and one that adopts an I CAN do it mindset, which Matt truly believes. Do you?

Brenda

Matt Evans

"Pain is temporary.
Mistakes can be rectified.
Paths can be altered.
Habits can be broken."
                    Matt Evans

My name is Matt Evans. I am an entrepreneur, a managing director, a business partner, a dad to five incredible children, a partner to a loving girlfriend (my rock), a mentor and now (scariest of all!) a public speaker.

Until January 2020, I was a total mess. A car crash. A liar, a cheat, an addict, a genuine selfish piece of work. I saw myself as a victim, as an abandoned child, a bullied schoolchild, a lost soul. I'd walked out on my children, lost relationships with my family, hurt anyone who came near me, and pushed away anyone that crossed me and everyone that knew me. I had a better relationship with my drug dealer than anyone I had ever known. I had no friends, just bad influence associates. I was contemplating my worth, and my existence, and I was done with the mess that I called my life...

But for some reason, something, or someone, was not done with me. Even at my lowest point, I always had the ignition still running. I always made sure I had enough petrol to start the engine again. I needed a wake-up call. I needed a miracle.

That came in the form of my girlfriend, Shannon. She is ten years my junior; she is stunning, she is my rock and she was and is to this day, my saviour. No one had ever stood up to me before. I was pretty bullish and always got my way. I couldn't achieve that with her and it had me all confused.

Why doesn't this one say, "Yes, Matt, OK, Matt, three bags full, Matt"? Why doesn't she accept finding me in a state, or a comedown, or peeping through the curtains in a state of paranoia? Why doesn't she do what everyone else does and just let me do my thing… Why?

It was because she was my saviour. Never in my life have I ever been so afraid to lose anyone before. She laid down the law. Stop doing what I am doing, or lose her and the baby (she was four months pregnant by then). Other people had said this to me before – even my own mum threatened to stop talking to me – but none were threatening enough. Shannon was.

On 23rd January 2020, I went for hypnotherapy for my 'Dad issues' (I'll come to that later) and my addiction, and I never looked back. No treatment, no counselling, no rehab; just stone-cold determination and willpower. Something I had never possessed before. I chose to change (with a little ultimatum and negotiation).

Since then, I have been trying to work out ways to help others. Although I needed a sustained period of successful abstinence before I became the preacher. But I did it.

The guy who would crawl around on the floor, in the rain, looking for the little chewing gum pot the dealer threw in the bush, the guy who spent more money on making his pain go away than his domestic bills, the guy who walked away from his three children because, at the time, that environment was never enough. He did it. He now stands up on stage talking about his past, helping others. He assists and offers incredible addiction solutions (infinity solutions) by taking phone calls from those that need his help. HE GOT BACK UP.

I'd like to take the next few paragraphs to go through my life experiences and lessons that led me to where I am today. Hopefully, this resonates with you. If it does, then my message was worth it. There will be something for everyone.

Give Yourself a Break

It is so easy to be hard on yourself, isn't it? "I'm an idiot", "I shouldn't have done that", "I can't do anything right"… blah, blah, blah. But really, we are victims of our own negativity, victims of our own selves all the time that we have not dealt with the things that are causing us the most pain. Give yourself a break. Look deeply at what your negative drivers are and ask yourself what would make that better. Look at the destruction that has been caused by allowing this to affect you and STOP. REFLECT. Realise that until you deal with the triggers, you are always going to be a mess. If there is anyone here, right now, that has just had a light bulb moment, then you have just taken the first step to be able to patch yourself up, dust yourself off, put a plan together and GET BACK UP.

Sometimes, we build up so much stress, so much anxiety, and so much fear that we will never change, that we are unable to recognise the things that are holding us back. STOP – give yourself a break. Take a few days off. Spend some time with your thoughts and make a plan. I would happily make myself available to help with the first steps – my details are at the back of the book. Rely on someone.

Don't do this alone. If you have no one, then reach out to me, or reach out to a professional support mechanism. Fear of change is a powerful thing and I appreciate how hard it is to ask for help, but you have to.

YOU CAN DO IT. YOU HAVE GOT THIS. YOU CAN GET BACK UP.

Every Day Is a Chance To Get Back Up

Pain is temporary. Mistakes can be rectified. Paths can be altered. Habits can be broken. I have spoken to so many people that have failed at recovery. I failed enough times myself prior to 2020. I would beat myself up and I would allow it to spiral me off track. I would feel guilty, I would be an emotional wreck and I would feel regret. But, today is a new day. What happened yesterday cannot be altered. The more time that we spend looking at all the things we did wrong, the more we are stopping ourselves from moving forwards.

If you caused someone pain, say sorry. It is never too late. It is not your choice that they forgive you, or how quickly they forgive you, but it is your responsibility to look them in the eye and say sorry, with sincerity. You must let them come round in their own time. The more you push and pressure, the less they will come to you. Let them lick their wounds with the knowledge that you are sorry, and time will do the rest.

If you make a mistake, then own it. Take responsibility for it, and put plans in place to rectify it. Try not to repeat history. Don't be alone. If you have taken the wrong path, made bad decisions and want to change lanes… then guess what? Change lanes! You can take whatever path that you want today. How you got here yesterday DOES NOT MATTER. It is where you go from now that defines you. If you have a habit that you cannot shift and you have already acknowledged that, then hats off to you. If there is anyone reading this book that thinks they may have an issue that they need help with, then reach out. Do it now; don't wait for fear to tell you not to.

YOU CAN DO IT. YOU HAVE GOT THIS. YOU CAN GET BACK UP.

Take It Slow

Research shows that breaking a habit may take anywhere from 18 to 254 days. The best ways to break a habit are by identifying your triggers, altering your environment or finding an accountability partner. Research also states that it takes up to 21 days to form a habit, and a further 90 days to implement that habit as a permanent lifestyle choice. So, it isn't easy and we know that. None of this will work if you don't identify the triggers that are causing you to feel the way that you do. This can be a painful process, but it is essential to your recovery. Take it slow. You may need help with changing the environment, or replacing the habit associated with the trigger with something more positive and less devastating, but help is there.

An accountability partner, sponsor or a friend/family member that is behind your recovery is an essential part of your success. You need them. Pick them wisely and let them know that by agreeing, they understand what is needed from them. No judgement, no fear of disappointing them. Just plain, simple support and understanding. Take your time. Once you have established these basic fundamentals, you can get to work on planning how you deal with the trigger.

Mine was my dad. He left when I was young; he was my absolute and total hero. I just wanted him to notice me. To call me all the time and tell me he loved me. To be there when I scored in my football matches, or to protect me from the bullies. He wasn't absent as such. I saw him physically, but I needed love and affection, and that wasn't his thing. He was a hard nut, an ex-football hooligan, a foster kid. He'd made it through his life without the emotion and affection that he wanted, so I guess he thought I could make it through my life the same. He was wrong.

I needed him more than he could ever imagine. All the way up to being an adult. At 37, I told him that I was an addict and that I needed him. He said, "Don't worry, son. I'll be there. I've got you". He never once checked in on me and I never heard from him in the way I needed. It broke my heart. That took time to get over.

Lockdown came and he told me to look after my wife (we'd been separated for months and I was isolating with my poor immune system and heavily pregnant girlfriend. He never once checked if we were OK). He told me to look after my kids (it was killing me that I couldn't scoop them up and tell them it would all be OK, but I had to protect the household I was in). He told me to do the things that he never did. He left my mum for another woman, set up home elsewhere, left us penniless and never told me he loved me. Yet, he was handing out advice. I flipped. I stood up to him. I told him what I thought of him. I never heard from him again.

YOU CAN DO IT. YOU HAVE GOT THIS. YOU CAN GET BACK UP.

Be Brave

I lost my dad, but it was the best decision I ever made. It gave me more strength than I realised that I had. I GOT BACK UP after 37 years of being on the canvas.

Scan the QR code below to see me, raw and emotional, dealing with the issues I have faced since my dad left, over 30 years ago.

YOU CAN DO IT. YOU HAVE GOT THIS. YOU CAN GET BACK UP.

Accept Your Past

This is tough. How do you accept your past, if the decisions you made in your past led you to some of the most painful and difficult times of your life? How do you put that behind you? How do you let that go? It isn't as hard as you think. You cannot change the past. Your wounds have healed, and you now have the scars, physically and mentally. But you also have the choice as to whether you let the past affect your future. You live for now, for tomorrow, for the future. You can't live for five minutes ago, or yesterday, or the last X years of your life. Because they are gone. Those moments, that pain, it doesn't need to follow you into your future.

Remember what we said earlier – every day is a chance to get back up. Every day is a new page in the book that is your life. It is up to you what you write – draw strength from the past. Use the experiences that you got over, that you moved on from, or that you left behind, to shape the new you. There is not one human on the plant that is Version One! I'd say I am Version 1,000,000 and I will keep adding to that!

If anyone reading this feels the significance of this message, then I encourage you to unveil the new version of yourself tomorrow. Give yourself the latest software update and grow. Our pain and our experiences teach us how to either handle the situation if it happens again, avoid the pain from resurfacing and become more resilient to adversity. I am grateful for my past. It has shaped my present and it is enabling me to set up my future. The past to me is my fuel. Let your past be yours.

YOU CAN DO IT. YOU HAVE GOT THIS. YOU CAN GET BACK UP.

Challenge Yourself Daily

Now that you have established the new you, it is time to push your limits.

Has anyone ever driven a car and legally (obviously) pushed it and pushed it to see how fast it goes, how quickly it accelerates, see how it handles? Exciting, isn't it? Well, this is exciting too! You have a new version of yourself to test out and you should be ready to see what is under the hood (hopefully not a dad bod like me)! Look for ways to challenge yourself every day. If you are a runner, run an extra km; if you are into weight lifting, do one more rep; if you are a salesperson, make one more phone call; if you are the top performer, ask for a promotion.

This new version of yourself needs to use all of the previous steps we have discussed to re-establish your self-belief. Bring back your self-esteem. Remember that only YOU are in control of your destiny and at times, you need to give yourself a pat on the back. Do something that scares you every day. Nothing that causes pain or puts you in danger, of course, but something that raises your adrenaline. Like standing up on stage in front of 1,000 strangers and hoping they don't think you are a total wally. You've come this far; now keep pushing and reach for the stars. YOU DESERVE IT.

YOU CAN DO IT. YOU HAVE GOT THIS. YOU CAN GET BACK UP.

Keep Going

You are going to come up against adversity again, only this time you can look at adversity and tell it to do one. You are equipped for that now. You are stronger, you are tougher, you are resilient and more than anything, You Know Your Worth. Remember to view all the life experiences that you endure as a lesson and there will be nothing that can hold you back. Just keep going. If you hit the canvas like Tyson Fury against Deontay Wilder, compose yourself and get back up.

In the words of Sylvester Stallone as Rocky Balboa from the *Rocky* films…

> *"Let me tell you something you already know. The world ain't all sunshine and rainbows. It's a very mean and nasty place and I don't care how tough you are it will beat you to your knees and keep you there permanently if you let it. You, me, or nobody is gonna hit as hard as life. But it ain't about how hard ya hit. It's about how hard you can get hit and keep moving forward. How much you can take and keep moving forward. That's how winning is done!"*

YOU CAN DO IT. YOU HAVE GOT THIS. YOU CAN GET BACK UP.

Understand Who You Are

One of my favourite quotes, which I first heard when watching the film *Coach Carter*, starring Morgan Freeman (GREAT film, by the way!) sums this up nicely…

> *"Our deepest fear is not that we are inadequate. Our deepest fear is that we are powerful beyond measure. It is our light, not our darkness, that most frightens us. We ask ourselves, Who am I to be brilliant, gorgeous, talented, fabulous? Actually, who are you not to be? You are a child of God. Your playing small doesn't serve the world. There's nothing enlightened about shrinking so that other people won't feel insecure around you. We are all meant to shine, as children do."*

You just need to accept yourself for who you are and for what you want to achieve. It is not your decision as to whether everyone accepts you. But if you act with integrity and be the best version of yourself, reaching for the stars, then you need have no fear.

You have the power to be whatever you want to be, whenever you choose to be it. When I was nine years old, I got hit by a car and I nearly lost my leg. I was told that I would have one leg shorter than the other, a permanent limp and I would NEVER play football again. I played as a semi-pro from the age of 19 to my mid-thirties. You have the power.

YOU CAN DO IT. YOU HAVE GOT THIS. YOU CAN GET BACK UP.

Be Proud of Yourself

You did it! You are doing your best. You are looking forwards. You are great. You should be proud of yourself. You took what the world had to offer and you keep moving forwards. You are here, ready and equipped for tomorrow.

YOU CAN DO IT.

YOU HAVE GOT THIS.

YOU CAN GET BACK UP.

"Strength doesn't come from
what you can do.
It comes from overcoming
the things you once thought
you couldn't."

Rikki Rogers

We are all energy; you certainly know Satwinder is in the room with his boundless positive energy. Having worked with Sat, I have felt the power of his energy and his determination to support others with whatever they need that day.

He is a true Samaritan. His story reveals that he is unique and he often unapologetically voices it. He believes in living authentically, and his path as an entrepreneur has challenged this way of being. A man of courage, he found the strength to ignore the naysayers and forge his path.

Sat is a man who is unafraid to share his stories and, as a true leader, encourages others to share theirs. His authenticity enables him to embrace his inner child, his love of *Mortal Kombat*, and all his walks on the road less travelled. He revealed his recent adventure into a woman's world and dived right into the world of menopause despite much criticism.

If you want to be inspired, then Sat's story will provide examples of how he lives his life being true to himself, no matter what others say about him. Go, Satwinder!

Brenda

Satwinder Sagoo

"The greatness we become is often what we greatly feared before we became it."

Satwinder Sagoo

Courage often creates the strength to be authentic, when your heart affirms the real you unapologetically. With a newfound conviction, you find the path to your destiny. Courage enables you to accept resistance, criticism and even haters when choosing your path. People will tear your building down to make theirs taller and even suggest you will never succeed. Your strength is never letting outside negativity interfere with inner strength and the enlightening journey you are walking. I want to share with you my story of the courage to be unique.

My courage flourished from my audacity to go against the grain in terms of my business and my image. I connected with my childhood pleasures and my experiences of heartbreak to create something truly magical and unique, resonating with so many on social media and in the real world. It is uncommon for people in business to show who they indeed are for fear of criticism from many with fixed perceptions of what makes a successful businessperson and coach.

This picture is my business photo and illustrates a bold idea. Most coaches dress smartly, smile and have nature as their background image – but that is not who I am. I chose to step right outside my comfort zone and be UNAPOLOGETICALLY ME.

So, where did this idea spring from? I'm a big fan of video games, mainly *Mortal Kombat*, and I am also a passionate martial artist, holding two black belts as a Second Dan black belt in Karate and a first Dan black belt in Jujitsu. My favourite character in *Mortal Kombat* is Raiden, a Thunder God with lightning powers, who is a symbol of strength, hope,and all that is good. He mentors his warriors, who are united to fight evil, and inspires them to see the wisdom and be a force both in training and in the war.

These traits resonate with me intensely, and I have been giving that same wisdom and energy to my warriors – my friends, family and business niche – for many years. Lightening is also my favourite source of nature as it represents power and energy.

I connected deeply with all those childhood passions to create the above theme with my business images and used the sci-fi electrifying lightning effect from my hands and eyes on the front cover of my book. I knew I was going against the status quo with a bold and daring brand.

Was it a wise move? Take a look at the following picture and judge for yourself. I pledge with my inner strength to be unique and stand in my power. This picture is my LinkedIn business profile which was used on the front cover of a prestigious global business magazine. I featured alongside 40 other global leaders, including Nick Vujicic, the inspiring international speaker born with no arms and legs. I knew I had made the correct decision when the

magazine publisher sent me a WhatsApp message telling me that it was the best front cover picture they had ever produced! It felt like I was giving the world power.

My book *Unleash Your Inner Power* is also an Amazon bestseller, a feat achieved within four weeks of its launch. When readers and potential clients look at my pictures, website or book, they tell me it permits them to step into their power. My brand and business image represent who I am, which attracts my tribe. When you consciously choose this intention, it provides you with a sense of purpose and fulfilment that is uniquely yours to fuel your mission.

Not only did I create a unique business brand, but a set of circumstances led me down the path of a subject matter pertinent to women – menopause. Synchronicity occurred, and several conversations later, I became a male Certified and Accredited Menopause Coach. This new path defies the status quo, and now my courage seems to be flowing through my veins. You would never imagine a man going public and talking about things such as periods, vaginal atrophy, breast tenderness and other significant symptoms during menopause, but that is what I do, and I do it proudly.

So, what led me to this unique and extraordinary path of stepping into a woman's world? Here is the story that started this journey…

Over three years ago, I was in a loving relationship with a fantastic woman who was my everything. We were each other's special one; though we lived two hours apart, the distance was no barrier to that love. In November 2019, I posted a social media post joking that I must regularly shave as I am becoming complacent in this department, to which she commented, "Why do you need to do that? I love you like crazy." Yet three weeks later, I was to witness a complete change of tone when I put a post celebrating her new phone upgrade, only to receive a comment from her that the photo was hideous. She also called me by my name and did not finish the statement off with any kisses — the first time that had ever happened. Straight away, I knew something was wrong.

She too was writing a book, which she was passionate about completing, and I gave her a few pointers. Out of nowhere, she snapped, "Am I not good enough for you?" This shocked me, and I had to get to the root of what was going on, so I showed strength and courage to suggest we both step back from the relationship to figure out what was happening. She agreed.

Whilst feeling sad and heartbroken, I still mustered up the strength to research what was happening. I learned that my ex was experiencing severe symptoms of menopause, which had a debilitating effect on her body and also caused drastic changes to her personality. As my understanding grew of this and I was relaying this information to her, we seemed to be slowly rekindling our love and affection, and I ended the year telling her I loved her. However, at the beginning of 2020, her personality changed again. She was cold and distant, and didn't even read my messages. My anxiety shot through the roof.

It was 9th January 2020. I was in a Jujitsu class and at the end of the class, I was shocked to find that both my partner and her daughter had blocked me from all their social media platforms, and it was the end of us as partners.

I was devastated and mortified, but I had to find the strength to move on, which I did, and I successfully launched my book only five weeks later, which then became an Amazon bestseller.

It is often the case that our most significant setbacks become our most incredible power. My heartbreaking experience was the platform that allowed me to do things very different from the norm, something unique. I started to be able to spot menopause symptoms in women very early and saw friends' relationships reach highly turbulent levels due to similar symptoms that my now ex-partner had experienced. I was a complete natural in making women and their partners understand their symptoms and work through menopause together.

I also learned that there were women who couldn't take HRT, who were completely against it or were being misdiagnosed by doctors. They needed a new mental

HRT source, so I developed POWER UP – a menopause positivity programme incorporating tools and techniques from my book to help women find their positivity during menopause. I am also developing a 'relationship rekindle' programme to help relationships thrive during menopause.

I have incredible testimonials of women in menopause whom I have worked with and helped find their positive power. The first of these was a woman in her early forties, who is four years post-menopausal and who is not on HRT. Her motivation was non-existent; she had shut herself away from social media for nearly two years and had an autistic daughter. Add to that the fact that she has childhood traumas of abuse, such as sexual abuse and being kidnapped, and those experiences are enough to make anyone break. However, when you align with your passion and purpose, you find the best version of yourself appears. This strong belief was evident as she re-discovered her positivity after five sessions with me, went back on social media, wrote her book, and launched her own coaching programme.

Another woman of a similar age traumatically split from her boyfriend. During this troubling episode, the local pharmacies ran out of HRT, which she relied on to alleviate her menopausal symptoms. This lack of much-needed medicine challenged her mentally and emotionally. Once again, I could use my experience, toolkit and training to work successfully with her. After five sessions with me, she found her positivity, started loving and valuing herself more, and went on holiday to begin her fantastic self-love journey.

Along the way, I have strengthened my mindset to ignore the naysayers and fortified my self-belief through training that benefits me with credibility, particularly as a man operating in a woman's world. I do not have the insight that a woman has, of course, but my experiences with menopausal women have enabled me to show empathy and compassion.

As a male menopause coach, I feature in many menopause podcasts and radio shows. I regularly speak about menopause at events and collaborate with several female menopause coaches to get a much-needed message out there.

I've shown the courage to have a creative sci-fi-style business photo representing me at my most authentic, and the courage to go against the grain of the norm and champion a woman's mid-life transition from a male perspective. What else could I do that was entirely against the norm and extravagant?

How about this...

I am now combining menopause and video gaming!

I write posts on social media and blogs on my website about menopause, and I often use video game analogies to highlight critical points. I found myself doing it naturally and authentically, using my favourite games such as *Sonic the Hedgehog*, *Halo*, *Street Fighter*, *Streets of Rage*, *Mortal Kombat*, *Skyrim* and *Call of Duty* to talk about menopause symptoms, mindset and communication. As a result of this uniqueness, my engagement shot up on LinkedIn, and I am receiving many collaboration opportunities.

How did I become so brave to be so different from others? My coach, Brenda Dempsey, who is also the author of this anthology, said one thing that has resonated with me...

"You must step out and be brave to stand out because that's what you were born to do, not fit in. Connect with your passions in life and bring them to your business."

That is why she is brilliant at what she does, because those words inspired me to find that authenticity and project it with pride.

A considerable part of business success is the courage to be REAL and purely YOU. That is how you start to enjoy all aspects of what you do in business and what helps attract your tribe. Having courage is stepping out to stand out rather than fit in. It is about accepting that you will feel resistance from some; you will also gain haters and people will try to destroy you to lift others and themselves, but you have a CHOICE – either listen to them or listen to yourself. Having this experience may be uncomfortable at first. Still, it is also positive as it shows that you are asserting yourself with YOUR values and beliefs rather than letting others mould you into whom they think you should be... after all, our life rules are up to us to create.

When you are living authentically, you never consider the competitive edge. There is enough for everyone, and for me, the only competitor I have is myself. I work consistently on myself, mentally and physically, and in so doing, I consistently improve myself.

As a new business owner, I seek support to lay solid foundations because I know that living a life of purpose will reward me abundantly in all aspects, personally and in business.

My resilience is extraordinary. In the face of criticism and adversity, I have the power to be a YES citizen in a huge NO society. I remember a time near the beginning of my entrepreneurial journey. This desire to write a book, speak on stage and make a difference in other people's lives was within me. Several business people turned to me and questioned who was I to write a book. I had no big following, no business and no idea where to start writing. However, I knew there were stories within me that illustrated the challenges I overcame. If they were essential life lessons for me, they would be helpful to others who experienced something similar. I heard many negative comments, but they can't keep a good man down, and my bouncebackability was my weapon to prove them wrong. I have a BIG heart, drive and willingness to learn. Today, I am so glad I took action and became a #1 bestselling author. If I can, you can too.

I have immense courage to step out and shine my unique authenticity in whatever way I see fit, without worrying about outside resistance and what others think I should be. I also dare to go against the grain of the norm and step into a world many others fear. I rise when others want to see me fall. But I have learnt that my inner compass keeps me going in the direction of my dreams. I have fallen in love with who I am, what I stand for and how I use my life to support and guide others. It is essential to be driven by compassion, understanding and a need to serve others, making me the man I am today.

I have the mental strength to believe I can move mountains and be extraordinary. My past success stories have all started from me visualising those happenings many months before they happened. I'd urge you to find your power of strength and then voice that strength so others can find theirs. Visualisation is a powerful tool, but it is more than just seeing a picture of what you desire. It's hearing the sounds and words, experiencing the feelings, making that picture bold and bright with as much detail as possible. If you have time, you can then journal that into your daydream journal, where you write about a day that is the best. Whatever rocks your world to better yourself, do it, for it will strengthen your inner resolve and allow you to climb any mountain.

Three tips to my younger self…

1. Be brave enough to stand up and write your own life story; never oblige yourself to give anyone your pen.

2. Know that it is OK to make mistakes; they are the most significant part of personal growth.

3. Be courageous enough to stand out – use your creativity to the max and entice the world to enjoy your show.

Here is a story not of a younger man and the trials and tribulations on our life's journey, but of a man who found the courage to choose a new path driven by passion. A man of faith, he listened to his inner God's voice to find the answers and took action on the message he received.

In life, there is a saying that when one door closes, another one opens. Belief and trust in this tenet catalysed moving forward on a new path that enabled Prof. Jagdish to live authentically, adding purpose and meaning to his life.

Awareness of your values enables you to make healthy decisions and ones that allow you to sleep soundly at night. Being driven by integrity is highlighted throughout this chapter, and Prof. Jagdish explains why it is prudent and wise to know the driving force of your life, as well as finding the courage to honour it.

Prof. Jagdish encourages you to follow your dreams and take action to make them come to fruition, regardless of your age or time. With determination to follow that dream, he describes his firm intention to become an author. He shares some of the content and beliefs in his book, *Who Am I? A Guide to Discover Your True S.E.L.F.*

Brenda

Prof. Dr Jagdish Khatri

"You can't be a good Human Resource unless you are a good Human Being first."
Prof. Dr Jagdish Khatri

There have been many occasions in my life when I have challenged the status quo and dared to chalk out an entirely new path suiting my passion. However, the first and biggest change was when after 26 years of distinguished service in industry with my engineering educational background, I decided to opt for voluntary retirement and switch over to the uncharted field of academics. At that point, I had 11 years of active service period left; my children were still in school and I had no appointment letter with me from any other organisation.

How did I find the courage for such radical change in my career as well as family life? Well, the sparking point was my love for academics and training. But, the courage was provided by my wife and children who supported my idea of taking voluntary retirement. They had as much faith in my capability to succeed as I had, or rather more than that.

I should mention one thing more here that gave me strength for transition. The day I was to submit my application for voluntary retirement, I couldn't sleep the whole night. In the early morning, I went to our nearby gurdwara to seek blessings from the Lord. I wanted to know what the Lord's wish was for me.

To my surprise, the advice from the Lord was very clear. It read, *"Jiske sir upar tu Swami, so dukh kaisa pave"*, meaning "How can a person face sorrow if he has your blessings?"

This strengthened my resolve to go ahead with my plans and make a transition for betterment. As I took the decision, the opportunity knocked at my door. A friend came to ask if I could support his institution in transition from a computer coaching centre to a management education college. That was the start of a new life, and it laid the foundation for a brighter career ahead.

It is a blessing as well as a choice to live an authentic life even amidst the prevailing competitive world. It demands absolute belief in self, faith in our beliefs and a heavy dose of perseverance. Spiritual wisdom comes to help in defining an authentic life and leading it. Authenticity requires being fair and transparent in our actions and having a certain degree of detachment from routine successes and failures. Peace of mind and purity of heart are essential requirements, as well as natural outcomes of an authentic life. Yes, it's not so easy to lead an authentic life in this competitive world where the parameters of success are defined in terms of the positions, power or riches you accumulate in life, without bothering about the means to achieve them. Yet, my belief is that at the tail end of life, what would matter most is not what we could obtain from life, but what we could **give back**. An authentic person is always conscious of the importance of high values and ethics and never compromises these for immediate gains.

Life never stops teaching if you are a good learner and observer. My life has also been full of such occasions that demanded inner strength of character. I had been serving in the position of Sr. Manager in the Purchase Department in heavy industry as my last assignment before I decided to opt out of the rat race. I was responsible for placing orders worth over 400 million rupees every year with Indian and overseas suppliers. There were pressures – some direct and some indirect – to favour particular parties for orders. At times, there were suggestions of seeking a fat commission from these parties for the payments being made. However, I was able to resist all such temptations and offers, owing to my religious outlook and the learning I had received from my parents. My wife and children were also of similar attitude towards honesty in life and never demanded anything more than what I was able to provide to them with my limited salary. This raised my strength level and helped me make the right choices.

The lesson I would like to stress here is that there are so many circumstances and occasions where you are asked to make unholy compromises; but if you have the spiritual values and support from family, you will come out stronger and unscathed from such circumstances.

Another big lesson that life has taught me is the importance of the power of dreams. Numerous instances of my life have been influenced by the intense aspirations and hopes I had. During childhood, I had the opportunity to read a magazine named *Soviet Union* published by the Russian government, at a municipal library near my home. I was fascinated by the pictures of Moscow, especially Red Square, and wished that someday I could be standing there.

After a lapse of over 45 years – yes, 45 long years! – I suddenly got an email from a senior professor at Moscow State University inviting me to attend and present my views at a global-level congress, named Globalistics–2015. I couldn't believe how he could find me and consider me fit for attending such a conference. Since then, I have been a regular visitor there and a popular speaker at conferences. The little knowledge I could get on learning the Russian language through the columns of that magazine has helped me a lot during my trips there.

Yet another example of the immense power of dreams is worth adding here. I always had a dream to be a celebrated author of books at international level. Judging from the presentations I used to make at various international conferences, one of my friends from Switzerland, Dr Zoran Vitorović, sent me a link to a reputable publisher from Latvia where I could submit my manuscript and get my book published without any publishing charges.

I was excited and penned my thoughts to write a book, *Discover Your S.E.L.F.* in 2020. The book was published and to my pleasant surprise, the publisher informed me that it was being translated into various languages. Now, my book is available in French, German, Italian, Polish, Spanish, Dutch, Bulgarian and Portuguese. I am not bothered about how many copies are sold. The fact that my book is considered worthy of being translated into so many languages is a big honour for me. I now have an Indian edition too, with the title, *Who Am I? A Guide to Discover Your True S.E.L.F.*

Another of my ambitions I had of having designations as 'Professor' and 'Director' was also fulfilled by the universe. After taking the plunge into the academic field and struggling for a few years, I got a part-time job at the prestigious University of Allahabad as Placement & Training Officer in the Psychology Department with the designation of Professor. A year later, I was approached by an upcoming MBA College to take charge as the Director, all without any effort from my side. I served for seven years as Director of that college, taking it to new heights.

Once again, I got an offer to be a Director of the Business Management Wing at a university without my even applying for it. With my connections established with senior professors at Moscow State University, I was able to persuade and establish a UNESCO Network Chair at this university and was named its Chair Holder.

All these kept happening without much effort from my end, proving the magical power of dreams...

To give my younger self tips to develop inner strength, my first tip would be: EXPLORE YOURSELF. Conduct a thorough introspection to explore various dimensions of your personality. What are your strengths? What are the areas you should improve? What are your dreams? What are your short-term and long-term goals? What is your value system? What attracts you most? What you would like to become? What is the importance of money in your life? What are your family liabilities? Who are your role models?

My second tip? KEEP LEARNING, KEEP GROWING! One of the most important aspects of life is to continuously explore areas of growth. It is said, "We do not GROW old; when we stop growing, we BECOME old!" Keep gaining new knowledge and adding to your skill inventory. My hobby of reading newspapers and magazines right from childhood has helped me a lot in my life. Even today, I spend one or two hours learning through reading books or online. I am proud to have maintained a large personal library at home.

My final tip is: HAVE FAITH IN YOURSELF: Without a strong faith in one's own capabilities and an unbeatable spirit of persistence, it is impossible to win over the challenges in one's life and career. Faith also means having a belief that whatever God has offered us in life is good for us and that whatever has not been provided was not necessary for us in the first place.

My favourite quote throughout life has been a couplet by the Urdu poet, Dr Allama Iqbal:

"Khudi ko kar buland itna, ki har taqdeer se pehle,
Khuda bande se khud poochhe, bata teri raza kya hai"

"Strive to reach such heights of excellence in your field
That even God has to consult you before writing your destiny."

This is the most inspiring quote for every individual, belonging to any field, and in any place irrespective of gender, age, ethnicity or status.

Another quote, coined by me, is:

"You can't be a good Human Resource
unless you are a good Human Being first."

This is important because I find too much emphasis being accorded these days to acquire technical skills and accomplishments of career success, ignoring the need for inculcating the right human values in character.

George is a fellow Scot, so we hit it off when we met to discuss his desire to write his memoir. George is a man of integrity and always does the best he can, no matter what he tries to do. Being immersed in a very male-infused career in the army from an early age, he abounds with respect for him and others.

In this chapter, George talks about leaving the army to forge a new path after 40 years of service. He shares his innermost thoughts about his transition from military life into a more commercial industry, especially the questionable attributes of some leaders. This discussion reveals who George is and what he stands for, and that meeting people with opposite characteristics soon had him questioning his position.

Sometimes, you must be like a salmon and swim against the tide. George, being true to himself, established his leadership style, which provided the rewards he needed to keep going. Leadership is about being a team player, and George soon found the tribe that enabled him to achieve the heights he was used to as an ex-serviceman. Now he was carving the same quality niche in civilian life.

One of George's greatest gifts is his high level of emotional intelligence. As a leader in today's world, it is necessary to have this level of self-awareness to show empathy to others. George's story is deep, resilient and infused with a Voice of Strength so others can follow their path.

Brenda

George Greig

"Leadership isn't about physical strength, individual capability, or supreme intelligence, but about having the character to influence and maximise the efforts of others towards the achievement of a goal."

George Greig

As a professional soldier and officer, I inhabited a male-dominated environment which taught me many life skills, not least to respect the fragility of life itself. I am also proud to state that it was never my ambition to take another life, whilst accepting that it might be required of me in battle during times of conflict. It is my genuine experience that such acceptance brings with it a realisation that life is very precious, and therefore every effort must be made to live and let live.

Throughout my military career, I was afforded many chances to help others, whether this was through participation in peacekeeping missions, war fighting to overturn dictators, or simply helping to improve the daily lives of people in the local communities in the areas in which I lived. I am grateful for such opportunities and believe that they have helped shape my attitude, behaviour, and respect for and tolerance of others, irrespective of their colour, creed or religion. It taught me to care for my fellow human beings. What struck me most as I went through life during these times, is that the majority of people are decent, kind and generous folk, who want to live their lives in safety, without stress or threat to their families, and with an ability to provide food and shelter for their loved ones. If these conditions are met, then the drivers for conflict are far less.

My personal desire has always been to be the best I can be, and to do so whilst being open, honest and transparent; I believe that by doing this, you allow people to see the real you.

As the 21st century approached, I knew that my life would change forever, as I had taken the very difficult decision to leave the services to find my feet in industry. I stepped into my first corporate job in early 2000 and was immediately taken aback at how driven certain managers and leaders appeared to be; whilst this did give me some initial comfort, as transitioning from a military to civilian lifestyle is quite challenging, the apparent lack of camaraderie, mutual respect and teamwork did alarm me somewhat.

It became increasingly more evident that this was a very different world and that for many, it was about themselves, and not the team. I didn't want to form immature impressions, but to me, everything is about 'the team', so I quickly decided that this was an area I wanted to address head-on, and that I was sure would add huge value to those around me.

As the first few years rolled on, I was often left astounded by just how insular certain people could be, and it seemed to be more prevalent as the players became more senior. "My way or the highway" was an attitude I simply did not understand, particularly so in high technology companies, where I had expected employers to want to harness the tremendous combined intellect and talent often available. The truth, of course, is that industry is more aligned to public thinking and behaviour than I had appreciated, and society sometimes expects certain behaviours; it's an environment where bullies often prevail and in which the fight for alpha male status is very much alive and well.

It was at this point in time that I started to realise that the ill-informed out there may well expect me to believe in this model, simply because of a badly skewed view of life in the army. Well, *that isn't me* and I made a very conscious decision to pursue my future career from the position my military training had delivered me into; building great teams, developing positive cultures in the workplace, managing from a position of mutual respect, and leading the growth, personal development and success of my staff. That's where I could make a difference, and that became my goal for the remainder of my working life.

This also fuelled a burning desire to show that compassion, care for others, inclusivity, and the will to do the right thing and do it properly, are basic requirements in the leadership and management game.

As a people-person, it had pleased me to find that workers in civilian life tended to respond well to genuine managerial interest in their feelings, performance and ideas. Strangely, mutual respect wasn't something that many managers seemed to care about, and it often felt that autocracy was more alive out of uniform than in it. My leadership style had never focused on physical presence or intimidation, and bullies are one of the things I have always hated most in life. I was definitely surprised by the JFDI (Just F***ing Do It) attitudes on display, but the reality is that was just a lack of ability on the part of these folk.

As I implemented my style across a range of large teams and groups, my resolve was continually strengthened by feedback from my employees. When a highly respected senior manager, with nearly 40 years' experience writes

"George is the best manager I have worked for," you know you are doing something right! In truth, that comment is as valuable to me as any report I received during my military career, and that is because of who wrote it and my respect for him as a person and professional.

Watching the individuals and teams I have led grow and succeed has provided a huge amount of personal satisfaction, not least because I believe these staff have gained true benefit from my first career. The relationships I have enjoyed mean everything to me, and many years after I left businesses, I maintain contact with so many ex-employees. I feel they are part of who I am, and they know I have their back, always.

I also know that I haven't done anything special, just applied the basic principles of leadership, but at the same time, I am proud that the staff that I have led have believed in me, and supported and respected what I have tried to do. I am truly buoyed by the quality of the people in our industry, and the very genuine care and professionalism they show on a daily basis. Supporting the emergency services carries a big responsibility and the part that industry plays is often overlooked, but not by the services themselves with whom outstanding partnerships have been formed. This has played a significant part in public safety over my time in industry.

The world of work is a competitive one and the simple reality is that we can't all be 'the boss', but that doesn't mean that we can't all make a difference; we absolutely can. It's a cliché, but being the best you can be is a very rewarding return on your personal investment; make your experience count by sharing it with others willingly. Seeing a protégé succeed feels incredibly rewarding, so give a little back. Always seek and build mutual respect at a personal and team level; it's immensely empowering to know that people care about you, and to care about others is a gift. Have your say, but always do so with a smile on your face because your competitors can sometimes be your best friends. Recognise the importance of diversity, inclusion and equality because the best person for the job is always the right appointment. Overcoming prejudice of any description is important, not just in the workplace, but in life generally. If tolerated, prejudice will grow and that will serve no good purpose. Above all else, I would advise anybody in business to remember, there is a life outside of work; don't forget to live it!

One of the most important things that I can take from my time in industry is the knowledge that any business which operates in an open, honest and transparent manner, is much more likely to succeed. The conundrum for me is that so many choose an alternative approach that, at best, is fraught with risk. My experience of clients is that you will secure their trust and confidence if you share the bad news, as well as the good. Teamwork can't succeed if one part of the team believes the position to be different from the others, so tell it as it is, and do so in a timely manner. Always remember, there is no 'I' in team.

I always say that you are only as strong as the weakest link, so don't wait to fail, identify that weakest link and focus on improvement. Nobody wants to fail and I guarantee that the vast majority of people will respond well to guidance, direction and mentoring. I think that Steve Jobs encapsulates this point perfectly in his quote *"Great things in business are never done by one person. They are done by a team of people."*

I realised the importance of empathy at an early stage of my working life, but as I grew older and gained experience, it became more evident that some people perceived it as a weakness; I find that sad. Over my years in industry, I met and worked with certain colleagues who simply didn't see the link to injury, illness or stress suffered by others as relevant to that person's performance at work. As with numerous things, this was not something I had seen in the vast majority of military leaders, where it was an inbuilt need to demonstrate care for your soldiers. As a consequence, I was surprised to see that level of selfishness and lack of understanding in a manager; it's even more shocking to say that I have experienced it at MD level. This is where the lack of leadership qualities has most disturbed me, and one has to question how that individual rose to such a position; I believe and will always maintain that your people are your number one asset.

Meeting the duty of care to the workforce is a key feature within a company's culture. People need to know that they matter, and building the mutual respect that I have alluded to previously is dependent on meeting that need. In many instances, good, clear, consistent communication is the difference between the staff having confidence that it exists or not.

In the COVID era, well-being and mental health have taken on a much greater meaning for everybody, and rightly so. In my opinion, this is one of the few positives to have emerged as a result of the pandemic, forcing employers to take wellness much more seriously. The application of much more proactive management in this area is essential, and I believe it will see many businesses build and develop a well-being/mental health capability internally. This level of care is essential in today's world, particularly as we seek to recover from the horrors of COVID, but also as we need to be seen to encourage better care of our mental health. This will not be the only lesson we learn, but it will be one of the most important, as I hope and believe that the bad old days of averting the full delivery of duty of care are behind us forever.

I took up my first leadership role as a junior soldier at the age of 16 and quickly started to understand that the journey from boy to man can be full of potholes in the road. As a consequence, I decided that it made sense to navigate it at a sensible speed; in other words, don't run before you can walk. I also realised that life constantly teaches us new things, so my three "top tips" would be:

1. Never consider that you know it all and be **wary** of those who do.

2. Always be **curious** and never be too proud to ask a question. Just remember the answer may not always be right.

3. There is always more than one side to a story, so seek out the alternative views and **listen** to them before making a decision.

*"Strength does not come
from the physical capacity.
It comes from
an indomitable will."*
        Mahatma Gandhi

My first conversation with Colin Tansley made me feel like I had a challenge. He was very eloquent in his communication, but soon his invisible guard dissolved to reveal the authentic Colin. Like most of us, we become a product of our environment, including the people we spend most of our time with. As an ex-copper, Colin had many questions; you could sense he needed to be sure he could trust you and that you were telling the truth.

In his chapter, Colin is open and honest, throughout the journey of becoming an author. As a man who lives by his values, he transformed from someone with an unconscious belief in himself, to someone who reflects awakened awareness and so melted the crispest of exteriors.

His story reveals how many people, especially men, go with the flow to be 'one of the boys' because it is easier than standing out and being principled. It takes tremendous guts to admit doing the right thing for you, showing a remarkable transformation in mind, heart and soul.

Colin has learned the most crucial lesson: that failures are lessons. As he walks a new path, many opportunities will open for him to explore, and he invites you to consider doing the same.

Brenda

Colin Tansley

"The best views come after the hardest climbs..."
Colin Tansley

A Recovering Cynic

One thing that working in a public services environment provides you with, is an innate sense of cynicism. There are many definitions of the word, but I quite like this one: *'An attitude of scornful or jaded negativity, especially a general distrust of the integrity or professed motives of others'*.

I remember being told by a serving cop prior to the joining the police service that I would become cynical. At the time, I thought nothing of it; I was young, coming from a services background. I enjoyed horseplay, the camaraderie and joking around. For the first couple of years, I eased myself from green to blue, though subconsciously I was changing. I became less trusting of people, wanted only to mix with my police colleagues and I fell in love with 'the job', as it is affectionately called, and at the expense of my children and family.

Only recently I compared two photos of my time in the police, that are about ten years apart. One is of me laughing and smiling in uniform and the other is of me as a Detective with what we called the 'stony face'. They could not be further apart in terms of the way I felt.

Whilst happy in my chosen career, I had become deeply untrusting of pretty much anyone outside of my work circle. Don't get me wrong, I have never regretted joining the police; it gave me a wealth of experiences, skills and knowledge, the like of which you just cannot get anywhere else. But there is a trade-off – you are exposed to the very worst of humanity, some of whom want to injure or even kill you. Factor in poverty, depravity and scenes you will never fully erase from your memory, and it becomes a heady mix. Because policing has an exciting side to it, it can also become addictive; adrenaline rushes are commonplace at public order incidents, vehicle pursuits, arrests and more.

Anyone that thinks this doesn't have an impact upon them as an individual and those close to them is kidding themselves. You only need look at the number of divorces, mental health issues, suicides and alcohol dependencies associated with police officers to get a small glimpse into the problem. I know many don't speak about it, as for the majority it would be seen as a weakness or letting the side down. It stays locked behind a barricaded door in the mind, but that doesn't mean it has gone away. However, I'm talking about it now and it was my own book *Mastering the Wolf* that provided me with the mindset and platform to do so.

I've always been a bit of a loner and have only ever relied on a small circle of friends. I'm happy with that, but there are, of course, times in your life when you must be part of a team, be that at work, sport or an ad-hoc team thrown together because of a life event. For example, a group of random strangers who must quickly bond together to solve a problem at a critical incident. If you end up in charge by design, or accidentally, then it is your role to provide the leadership and formulate the values of the group. If you are a newcomer and join the team, it is often much easier to adopt the values and ethics of the group, to fit in rather than challenge them. Most of the time, we go with the flow; it's a human trait and there are times in my life when I have done exactly that.

To do the opposite and challenge 'group think' can be extremely difficult and you run the risk of alienating yourself or being identified as a troublemaker. With my background in the disciplined services (the army and the police), you did as you were told; woe betide you if you questioned 'orders'! That's not to say I haven't done it, sometimes out of blatant mischief as a young soldier and much later in life, particularly if I felt strongly about something, then I would speak out. Much of the time, it was easier to have a moan amongst your friends, family and colleagues though. Police officers are specialists in the art of moaning.

In *Mastering the Wolf*, I recount some of these issues. I didn't think that drinking and socialising were the right thing to be doing during work time when in the CID, but I went along with it. Why? Because all the people I was working with did it. It was almost a tradition and had been going on for many years. Did I ever think to challenge it? Of course not, I was enjoying myself, and it was easy to maintain the status quo. Other than our uniformed colleagues, who knew full well what was going on and grumbled about it, I do not know of anyone that ever questioned it openly. I am, however, aware of individuals that challenged the 'culture' of the police service and were ostracised as a result. Why do I mention this? Because seeing how they were treated reminded me it was just easier not to stick your head above the parapet.

My initial objective was to write a manuscript for my children and grandchildren, the intention being to leave them a legacy about me, my life and my experiences, in the hope that it might help them in their individual life journeys. I then decided I would self-publish using a pseudonym with the book redacted so as not to identify anyone, me included.

I then met Brenda from Book Brilliance Publishing. As part of what she calls the Author Journey, she asked me on several occasions whether I would consider releasing *Mastering the Wolf* in my own name. It was a hard no for many weeks; I wasn't prepared to disclose aspects of my personal life to the world! But one word kept cropping up in our discussions, and that word was 'courage'. The courage to write a book in the first place, but also the courage to be prepared to stand, front and centre, alongside it.

One morning, I woke up and decided I was being less than courageous not to put my name to what I had written. I took a breath, sent a text to Brenda and told her that we should be open as to who the author is. It was a pivotal moment for me. Some years earlier I had fulfilled a lifelong ambition of completing a parachute jump, and I likened it to that, leaping off into the unknown. I did not know what the outcome would be but was prepared to take it on the chin. I was stepping out of the shadows.

Like that parachute jump, there were feelings of elation and excitement associated with writing my book, particularly when I received the first printed copy and held it in my hand. There was fear too; I didn't know what people would think of me. I had always been – pardon the pun – a closed book. Putting myself 'out there' wasn't my thing, I had always preferred to be in the background, always working hard, but behind the scenes. Through the process of writing, engaging with my publisher and the marketing, I became more aware that I had something to offer. I had a voice, was authentic and could speak with authority. Working for myself allows me considerable freedom, which I cherish and am grateful for. That allows me the space not to follow the herd. I have built my business around trust, integrity and security. I choose who I want to work with. Unless they share my values, then it is never going to work, and I have several examples of removing myself from business relationships that stepped outside of my boundaries.

I have learnt so much since publication. I know much more about me and how my life journey has shaped me as an individual. I have taken the time to explore how the mind works and the techniques that can be adopted to calm the brain. I think differently and have a more positive outlook on life. Because of the book, I have met and spoken to so many different people therapists, counsellors, to readers who frequently say, *"Your book resonated with me"*. That suggests, to me anyway, that many people suffer in silence, are prepared to 'live with it' or fear disclosing their own experiences. It is only by being brave enough to speak out that things will change.

If there is one thing I have learnt about being a man living 'authentically' in a very competitive world, it is to be prepared to show your human side. My prior training and the work I chose to be involved in had a culture of 'grin and bear it', 'man up' and a whole host of other, unprintable phrases. There is, of course, a place for that type of mindset;

you cannot, for example, show up to a traumatic incident and break down. You develop an outward facing exterior to deal with it – we used to call it the 'blue light force field'.

The problem, as I see it, is knowing when to step out of that exterior and be yourself again. Like many of my colleagues, I normalised and embraced the 'macho' habits until it suppressed my emotions. There is a time and a place to be emotional and everyone has their way of dealing with it. I enjoy watching films and a wide genre of TV series. There are times when they make me sad. I have no problem now to cry in front of my wife, an amazingly supportive, caring individual whom I trust without question. I also talk much more openly about my feelings with her, my children and my grandchildren. They deserve to see that side of me.

Don't get me wrong, I questions things, I speak my mind, I work hard and I still have an entrenched value system. The difference now though, rather than 'react', is that I 'respond'. I want to hear the other point of view and like to challenge my thinking. I still refer to myself as a 'recovering cynic' but that part of me is shrinking, although it will never disappear, and I am not sure I ever want it to. My work does still call for me to be suspicious, but it is under control now, reserved for the investigations I conduct and discussed during the training I deliver.

Where do I go from here? I really don't know, but neither am I so wrapped up in controlling the outcomes. I have plans, but I am also happy to go with the flow. I do know I am on a different path; I've reset with new ideas, have re-evaluated and am committed to enjoying life without being so wedded to work. I've seen too many of my friends and colleagues suffer from poor physical and mental health, some unable to detach themselves from their service days. As you grow older, you begin to realise just how short your life is. No one is going to remember how much you earnt, what possessions you had or the size of your house. What they will remember is how you made them feel. It is my hope then that writing *Mastering the Wolf* and contributing to *Voices of Strength* will help someone, somewhere.

The three tips I would give to my younger self to develop inner strength are:

- Life is one big classroom; learn to listen, listen to learn.

- Have confidence in your own ability; be yourself.

- Don't view mistakes as failures; treat them as lessons.

"Out of your vulnerabilities will come your strength."

Sigmund Freud

Matt has great insight into who he is, and his chapter's very title begins with the driving power within him. He is a modern man driven by Values. Lessons have taught him what it takes to live authentically and you will be surprised that it is not the mountain you think it is, but having the plan to share your brilliance. His inner journey led him to understand that he is in control and that finding the courage to say NO to the conventional norms of society was the catalyst he needed to change.

Matt's story is straightforward and defines each aspect he has used to determine who he is and why he serves others. Ultimately, it is about teaching the reader through lessons learnt that provide steps that encourage action. In his unwavering fashion, he has gained insight into what it takes to live authentically and uses these lessons to create the change he needs to be the best version of himself.

Brenda

Matt Mo CVO

*"Don't choke on your
decision, you're allowed to
have ambition."*

Matt Mo CVO

VALUES
My Journey to the Guiding Principles
Of My Life as a Modern Man

Being a man in the 21st century can seem like a complex and challenging task. It is not just about following the status quo, but about having the courage to change your mindset, your words and your actions in order to live an authentic life. True integrity means being accountable for your actions and taking responsibility for their consequences.

The pivotal moment for me came when I realised that the traditional concept of masculinity was not serving me well. I was often striving for success and validation from others. I was caught in a toxic cycle of trying to live up to societal expectations of what it means to "be a man".

With this newfound understanding, I began to make changes in my life. I had to examine my own beliefs and values, to determine if they were truly in alignment with who I am as a person. This transition was not easy. It required a lot of self-reflection, introspection and courage. I started to prioritise my own personal growth and fulfilment. I focused on developing my own values, rather than trying to conform to the values of others. I began to practice self-discipline, compassion, responsibility and spiritual awareness. And I started to surround myself with people who supported and encouraged my growth and development.

My contribution to this book is a personal journey of self-discovery, where I share my experiences and reflections on what it means to be a strong man in today's world. I will explore the values of honesty, integrity, reliability, decency, sustainability, highest quality, responsibility, consistency, solidarity and equality, and how they have shaped my understanding of true strength.

These values helped me become a better person and a better leader on the foundation of self-discipline and compassion, supporting me in finding spiritual awareness to be an important aspect of being a strong man. I discovered the power of mindfulness and meditation in helping me to stay centred, grounded and in touch with my inner self. It helped me to release negative emotions and to focus on the present moment. Through spiritual awareness, I found inner peace and a deeper understanding of myself and the world around me.

Too often, we allow negative emotions to get the best of us and generate negative energy, impacting us in the most toxic way. The human mind, body and spirit work in this order:

Thoughts > Feelings > Actions > Results

Knowing this, we must understand the extreme importance of controlling our thoughts and staying in control of them, ideally at all times. Another person or some situation beyond our control should never ever be the centre of our thoughts, as they are the essence of everything we feel and do. Only one person shall have this power over you and that is YOURSELF.

It is important to understand though that coming to this realisation and practising staying in control of one's own thoughts is indeed a process. This does not happen overnight and requires continuous efforts, reminding yourself of the importance of keeping control over your thoughts. With time, you will become stronger and better at this, until it is a natural and automated process in your mind.

The following values are the guiding principles that shape my decisions and the way my team and I work at my companies. They are also the foundation upon which I built my life and they determine the kind of person I aspire to be.

HONESTY

We must always speak the truth, no matter the consequences. Honesty has to be the basis of absolutely everything we say and do every day. Honesty is the foundation of all relationships, both personal and professional. It is the cornerstone of trust, and without it, all other values are meaningless. Honesty is about being true to oneself and others, and about being transparent. There should be zero tolerance for dishonesty in our personal and professional lives.

INTEGRITY

Compromising moral and ethical principles has to be a no-go. We must have an extremely high sense of fairness and regard having a strong backbone as a virtue. Integrity is about living in alignment with one's values and principles.

It is about being true to oneself, even when it is difficult or uncomfortable. It is about standing up for what is right.

RELIABILITY

What we say we are going to do, we have to do. Commitments we make, standards we implement, follow-ups we promise – should be considered as done by others. We need to always continue to establish a culture of over-delivering. Reliability is about being dependable and trustworthy. It is about following through on one's commitments and delivering on one's promises, being there for others when they need you, and about being dependable in all aspects of life.

DECENCY

Especially if we operate a business, we have to value decency over profits. We would not sell a product or service not suitable to a client's needs, just so we can make a profit. We are looking to build customer relationships for life. It is about being considerate of others' feelings and needs, and about being sensitive to their perspectives. Decency is about being compassionate and empathetic, and about being a good listener. It is about being a good person, and about treating others with the same kindness and respect that we would like to be treated ourselves.

SUSTAINABILTY

Planet Earth is our home, and we must protect it. Looking after our environment needs to be a routine for us – at home, in our offices and in everyday life. As little trash as possible, no unnecessary plastic, no overproducing. Sustainability is about preserving the natural environment for future generations. It is about being mindful of the impact that our actions have on the planet, and about taking steps to reduce our carbon footprint and conserve natural resources. Sustainability is about living in harmony with nature, and about being responsible stewards of the earth.

HIGHEST QUALITY

Whether it's about communication, content or care, others should expect absolute peak performance from us. No less than "best in class" is the standard we set for ourselves. The highest quality is about striving for excellence in all aspects of life. It is about being dedicated to continuous improvement, and about being committed to achieving the best possible outcome. It is about being detail-oriented and about taking pride in one's work. It is about being committed to excellence.

RESPONSIBILITY

Dealing with human beings and helping educate them is a huge privilege. We must take that privilege very seriously. Ensuring the well-being of our customers, mentally and physically, is how we operate. Responsibility is about being dependable and trustworthy, and about taking ownership of one's mistakes.

CONSISTENCY

World-Class Events – over and over and over and over. We never stop improving. For every event we do, we put all effort into it to make it even better than the previous one. Standing still is not an option for us.

SOLIDARITY

If our help is needed, by human or animal, we will be there. We do not care why or how a situation became problematic. Our focus is on the solution, not the problem. The secret to living is giving. Solidarity is about standing together with others in support of a common cause. It is about being a good ally, and about being supportive of those who are marginalised or oppressed. Solidarity is also about being there for others and about being a good listener.

EQUALITY

One World, One People. We do not believe in boundaries or limitations about gender, age, race, skin colour, ethnicity, sexual orientation, political beliefs or anything else. We are open to anyone's opinion and while we may not agree, we will listen and try to understand everyone's view, as long as it's based on the principle of democracy. One of our leading principles is "seek first to understand, then to be understood". Equality is about recognising that every person has inherent worth and value, and about treating others with the same kindness and respect that we would like to be treated with.

In addition to the above-mentioned values, I would suggest to my younger self the three following principles on how to tackle life:

1. Be true to yourself

Don't try to be someone you're not. It's important to understand that we are all unique and that we should embrace our individuality.

2. Live a life of authenticity and passion

True strength comes from living a life that is authentic and true to oneself. Find your passion, and figure out what makes you jump out of bed in the morning. Do what you love and love what you do. Anything else will not give you a life of feeling fulfilled. Always be the best version of yourself. Tomorrow, you should be better than you were today.

3. Don't chase money

In today's competitive world, it's easy to get caught up in the rat race of success and validation. Don't allow money to be in the driver's seat, don't allow money to be your motivation. Money needs to be a side-effect of what you do.

But please don't get me wrong on the topic of money, I'm not one of those people who will tell you "money doesn't buy you happiness". That is an incorrect interpretation of the purpose of money; it was never designed to make you happy and such silly statements are usually made by people who don't have any money. They are not the ones you should be taking financial advice from. It's like taking relationship advice from someone who has been divorced four times...

However, the things you can do with money are surely designed and able to make you happy. What those things are, is for you to figure out. It can be a nice home for yourself, it can be early retirement for your parents, helping to feed doggies at your local shelter, building a school for children who were not lucky enough to be born into a wealthy society, and anything else that will give you a sense of accomplishment and achievement.

The fashion designer Karl Lagerfeld once said, *"You must throw money out the window, in order for it to come back in through the door."* I strongly agree with him and the level of success he achieved in his life speaks for itself.

It's important to remember that being a modern man is not about being perfect. It's about being true to oneself, and willing to grow and learn from our experiences. It means having the courage to break away from societal expectations. With that mindset, we can be the best version of ourselves and make a positive impact on the world around us.

Values are the foundation upon which we build our lives, and they determine the kind of person we aspire to be. They will help us gain the wisdom to know when to change our mindset, words and actions, for that is the true measure of a strong man.

A man who walks his talk, exudes empathy and is passionate about serving others, Eric Francis has designed his life to allow him to be true to himself. A family man, Eric knows well the challenges men face in business, deciding whether to meet his family's or business's needs first. He shares with the reader how he manages these tough decisions, making him feel at ease with his choices.

His journey has led him to focus on men's mental health, particularly from the perspective of people in business. He blends the old and the new to create something different, using innovation to drive his ideas forward. Eric shares some of his traits and strategies to keep him in high energy and to avoid distractions, which in today's world, with all of the technology at our disposal, is challenging. Enjoy reading his story, and I know there will be ideas within the following pages that will inspire you to try the same.

Brenda

Eric Francis Manu

*"Change Yourself,
Change One Person,
Change The World."*
                  Eric Francis Manu

My name is Eric Francis Manu.
I am an award-winning entrepreneur, TEDx speaker and executive coach of Ghanain heritage.

I love to work in the business world to empower people to be their best in their chosen fields. My work is mainly with international companies in the corporate world, where my experience lies. Work/life balance is tricky because I have young children. However, I love the challenge of combining everything: contracts, projects and family time. I use my inner compass and do my best, especially when I feel time-poor.

There is more to being a man in the 21st century than following the status quo; the world tells you how you should behave as a man. But I think in today's world, we are beginning to sit up and notice how we work, as many people realise it's unrealistic, given the pressures that we face in the modern world.

I have recently been focusing on men's mental health challenges. We speak about mental health more, but it will take some time to understand its implications for individuals and society. I believe we play our part in changing this perspective because the expectations from society on men impact their level of happiness.

One of the issues men have is many are ego-driven and think they can, or even have to, do it alone. This unconscious self-imposed pressure manifests in issues around their mental health. Frequently, they watch the clock trying to get everything done. Sometimes, I drink four or five cups of coffee a day, which is unsuitable for my health. Working in this way creates and takes high energy, which is dangerous for your overall health and well-being.

What if we turned this notion and expectation on its head and slowed everything down, instead of focusing on everything sped up? Remember the old proverb:

"More haste, less speed."

In today's world, this expresses itself in areas of physical and mental health. When you slow down, you realise you have more time to focus on yourself, your duties and your mental health, allowing you to release the stress and get more done. Often we believe we get more things done if we rush, which is not always the case. So a light bulb moment for me was learning to slow down. I concluded that I could change as a man, an individual and a human by focusing on how I feel and the impact on my mental health.

Over the years, my philosophy has evolved from many experiences, expertise and education. I express it like this: **change myself, change one person, change the world**.

One of my aims asks, "How do I change my approach in dealing with people?" I apply this to my team, as a father and to society. There is a famous phrase we say in Africa: "A little drop of water makes a mighty ocean." My understanding is that if my input can change one person, then it can also change society, and that society can then change the world. Therefore whatever I do and the energy I put into something enables me to make a difference in the world.

When you have something you deeply believe in, that shapes your philosophy. It becomes like a mantra or belief that's deeply rooted in your inner journey at a soul level. It's about being unafraid to go on this inner journey.

As a man, I believe we try to be overachievers and do not consider the impact that has on ourselves and others. Centuries of limiting beliefs have fed us false information but once we awaken to something that stems from the inside, we realise we need to love and give more to ourselves, our children and our families. We have to stop the flow of unconsciousness drifting, otherwise we are continuing to be consumed by all things that negatively impact us, leading to serious mental health issues. Awakening our conscious being will enable us to shape more positive philosophies, be more optimistic and live happier, more fulfilled lives.

The courage to change begins with mindset. I believe that whatever you set your mind on, you can achieve. Every year in January, we set resolutions. We think about what we want to achieve in the year ahead. However, within a few weeks, that goal dies. The reason for this is that we lack the zeal to go the distance. We are not connected to the outcome in a way that fuels the drive necessary to achieve long-term goals.

It takes energy and willpower to focus on changing your thought patterns and it's important to know that it doesn't happen in a month or two; breaking patterns and setting up new ones takes time, effort and belief.

When I consider what it takes to make the change, the word I come back to is courage. You need courage to try something new, stick to something and make a difference because the world is quick to knock you down. Use your courage to do it differently, go against the grain and ignore what others say. Then listen to your inner voice and ignore the noise that others make to try and change your mind so you are more like them, rather than stepping into your highest value or best version of yourself. Let courage talk to your mind to provide the focus and dedication needed to achieve whatever you set your mind to envision.

I have this 'thing' that I have to complete one project before I begin another one. My mindset is so focused on that activity or project, that it has no room to take on something else that requires more thought processes, so I refuse to start something new. One of the other elements you have to develop is the sense of dedication to one thing. That way, you can get things completed to a high standard and in a professional way. When you sharpen your mindset in these ways, you can achieve your goals more frequently. With laser focus, there is less risk of being distracted or interrupted, and you remain true to your word. All of this deep personal achievement lifts your level of self-belief, worth and confidence; I often say Mindset – Achievement – Worth.

When I take on board a project, I want to do it the right way, be authentic and creative, all wrapped up in working towards a deadline. I think we become better when we stick to deadlines rather than being vague. This allows procrastination and distraction through a slightly open door, whereas a deadline has no room for any of these interruptions. Taking it a step further involves a commitment to yourself and your goals. I have established that authenticity is vital to your success, and I also believe faith in yourself is just as crucial.

Over the last couple of years, I have become a gym person. I love to regularly go to the gym as part of my health routine. Just like in my professional life, I set myself a target and goals to achieve my desire. Of course, there are days when I think it too much of an effort but I remind myself that I have set a goal I must achieve because I want to be the healthiest version of me. Like all goals, there has to be focus and dedication so I remind myself of my philosophy. I cannot argue with that which will create the best version of me for my life, family and world.

To be a man living authentically in a competitive world, you have to define and understand what we mean by this. My industry, coaching, is competitive because everyone is striving to be the best that they can be. Everyone wants to be the go-to expert, the number one in their field. However, I feel you have to be authentic and always true to yourself, because you are unique. There is only one of you and you bring your own learning, experiences and personality to the table for others to connect and resonate with so they can move forward and learn from you.

There is a quote by the great motivational speaker Jim Rohn that inspires me:

> *"If you don't design your own life plan,*
> *chances are you will fall into someone else's plan.*
> *And guess what they have planned for you? Not much!"*

When I focus on being true to myself, I can continue achieving small steps to reach my highest self, to serve others; the true purpose of why I am here on earth. I believe this perception is how you eradicate competition. I will do whatever I can to inspire everyone, including the next generation.

We have to be true to our inner self, our soul and our mind. I work with many of the top personnel in their industries and you can easily tell they are fuelled by beating the competition. I have to rise above that and keep true to my values and principles, no matter what they choose to do. It always comes back to being the best I can be. If I were to choose to follow them and their values which did not reflect mine, then that could be a dangerous slippery slope. The challenge of competition is to stay true to your values and principles, and not be tempted by the idea that popularity is the goal.

I choose not to believe in competition, but prefer to believe in **collaboration** with others. However, I am competitive with myself. I have to be better tomorrow than I am today, and better today than I was yesterday. So competition lies within me to better myself.

My strength is resilience. I embodied resilience from an early age.

I lost my mum when I was very young; my younger sister was only five at the time. After my mother's passing, I became the breadwinner. We had to leave private school and go to a state school instead. At that point, I became resilient in my thinking; I had to be for my sister and family. That shocking experience of death at a young age leaves you with a sense that you have to be resilient to survive. You have a job to do and as I have said all along, not just any old job, but the best job. I was the oldest in my family, so became father, mother and the 'man' of the house, with responsibility. When you are in this position, you quickly learn to develop critical thinking because you have to take decisions about someone else's life.

This experience is not penalty-free because it often comes back to haunt me. Being so responsible for my brothers and sisters, I feel I was robbed of some of my essential childhood development. I realised that I have suppressed my emotions and now I have to work on that aspect of me for the sake of my own children and my life. So resilience runs through my veins as a way to keep going.

When I stepped into my teenage years, I adopted a tougher approach to life and was less emotional. Whilst it is important in life to be resilient, it can often lead to living automatically without emotion. It is vital to face your emotions, accept them and deal with them to truly become emotionally resilient and lessen the impact on your mental health. I have developed a toughness, especially relating to my mindset.

I have a drive toward education and I absorb it and I deliver it because I believe it can help you develop a tough, resilient mindset. I love to share strategies that can help others deal with problems and situations but I am mindful that my youth has left me in a drought of emotion. As a man, father and husband, the awareness allows me to develop that area of my life which can only benefit me and my business.

Another valuable lesson is finding the courage to be vulnerable. You might be tough and resilient in many areas but you may be lacking emotionally – it is about being aware of not just your talents and gifts, but those areas of your life that need developing. Sometimes we worry in case we give people the wrong signal. For example, someone might share that they have lost their mum or dad and you respond, "I am sorry to hear that," and then move on. You have demonstrated understanding on one level but have not taken it to the next by continuing the conversation and asking them how they are feeling. I think that I don't show emotion because I believe I have dealt with it by creating a strong, resilient mindset, but sometimes the toughness acts as a shield for my feelings. We learn to bury them for years and years.

When I consider my emotional connection to people, I don't necessarily think it is as connected as it might be, which can then blur perceptions. I often wonder if people think I don't care. This is not the case; it's just that the pain of losing a parent is difficult for me to express emotionally.

Therefore it is about being prepared to be vulnerable, because you worry about how it will impact you and so you feed the fear and continue onwards without addressing the issue. But when you decide to be vulnerable, to build that emotional resilience, you will grow in stature and confidence. Only then can you begin to understand what it might be like to walk a mile in someone else's shoes.

I believe men are good at building tough mindsets and equally good at shutting down emotional responses out of fear of showing vulnerability and being considered weak. But it is the **opposite**; it shows strength to be vulnerable, authentic and open, and there is the wisdom of experience and a knowing that emerges from your inner strength. You become armed with a Voice of Strength to speak out. I encourage you to always be true to yourself inside and out.

We sometimes need to ponder on our backgrounds and the era we were brought up in. African cultures are very strict and the expectations on you as a male are huge. This has been the way of life for hundreds of years and until the younger generations are strong enough to seek change, it continues. I believe as the world gets smaller and we have access to more information, education is playing its role in the demand for change. In years gone by, boys were told, "Big boys don't cry," as tears were a 'girl' thing and showed weakness. As we learn more about emotions and their impact on our mental health, we know it is time for change. Now we see men crying quite openly; I feel this is progress for humanity. I believe that it is important for men to show their sons that being vulnerable is human. My life experiences have taught me to express my emotions, talk it out and cry. Whether you are prepared to cry in public or not, that's something you can work through but definitely take yourself to your room and let the tears flow. That is the real strength.

Overall, I have learned that we need to nurture our mental health and look after it well, so I would tell younger Eric to take it easy and have fun. Enjoy life and embrace all of its emotions. Have a day to laugh and a day to cry. Make sure you have balance in your emotions to keep your mind healthy.

Secondly, I would tell younger Eric not to set such high expectations that will disappoint him should he not achieve them. It is our energy force to want more and aim high, but be realistic in those aims and take them one small step at a time rather than trying to leap at every opportunity. I see it as going to war with the wrong weapon. It is about finding the right approach. Sometimes when we are young, we are focused on the big car, house and money, rather than the traits that make us great human beings.

Lastly, I would say open up and talk to people. Do not keep everything bottled up inside because you are building a pressure cooker and you know what happens when it gets too much – it explodes. Seek help and find a mentor, someone you can trust to whom you can open up and speak to about anything. Fear not being judged, for that will hold you back. Know that openness sets you free.

And finally, share your story, for there is someone out there who needs to hear it.

When you meet Kevin Ward, you can sense his inner power and commitment to humility, diligence and being proactive. He has lived a life entrenched by rules and regulations working in the construction industry. Kevin's story is honest and teaches the power of learning the value of introspection at the unlikeliest of times. It takes courage to go on an inner journey because you have to face yourself, warts and all. In modern times, this can be particularly challenging for men.

Kevin's chapter explains how life can take you on a different path and that road less travelled has many lessons and gifts which equip you for tomorrow. The most extraordinary relationship is with yourself, the one Kevin chooses to share in *Voices of Strength*. Finding that inner strength, resilience and truth leads you to recognise the wisdom you have gathered on life's journey and use it to benefit others. Kevin shows you how to embrace that inner teacher, voice and leader so that you can inspire others to do the same. Enjoy this heart-warming and honest story, and perhaps you might recognise yourself.

Brenda

Dr Kevin Ward

"Leadership is the actions and attitudes displayed by one individual while reaching their full potential, that inspires others to reach their full potential as they both pursue a shared vision."

Dr Kevin Ward

Adventure Into Healing

Cocky rooster???!!! What's up with that? I came to realise that's what I was back in the eighties. I know, that still doesn't explain it, does it? You see, I thought of myself as very confident and capable of not being outdone or outsmarted by anyone. I was indeed capable, and I also thought I was reasonably humble too... Interestingly enough, when interacting with many people I was fine and could defer to them and their opinions. I could engage in reasonable give and take, even though I had strong opinions. Some considered me a bit cocky but not obnoxious and even nice. But...

I found at some times that when I would engage some people with strong personalities, I had to be right! I thought I was right, so I had to prove I was right. Sometimes, even if I agreed with these people, I still had to find something to be right about... I know, sounds a bit crazy! At the time, I just thought, "I'm right, so it is only appropriate for me to demonstrate it." It wasn't a matter of 'pride' – it was just that I was right. So why not prove it via dialogue which usually involved debate and even arguments, even when I agreed? Hmm, at the time, I just thought some of these people were stubborn and really didn't want to learn... after all, I was right.

The final straw was at work... One of my co-workers, named Ed, and I couldn't be in a room together more than about five minutes before we were debating or even arguing about something, almost anything... There were indeed even moments when we would become disagreeable even when we agreed. Then one day our boss called me in and explained that Ed was getting promoted ahead of me! What!!!??? It blew me out of the water... When I sought the counsel of friends and family, they suggested that I might need to look inward...

So, what happened? How did I come to terms with this situation? I would like to say I was such a thoughtful and insightful individual that I recognised what was wrong and just went about fixing it. Fortunately, I had people around me that cared enough to be honest, then some life situations got my attention. Last, but certainly not least, I have a Heavenly Father that is involved in my life to help me grow when the time is right. I realised that the problem was... ME!

This started a process... a process of introspection, pain, and healing... I began to see, see, and feel a wound... a wound that was captured in an incident in my life when I was 13 years old. I can still remember it vividly as if it happened yesterday. An incident where I was looking for affirmation as a developing young man, affirmation from my father. Not only did I not get the affirmation I needed, but I felt rejected and dismissed... At the time it happened, I stowed it away... deep inside... so far that I forgot about it.

Moving forward by taking responsibility, I connected the dots between my former hurts and my current behaviours and realised that it was now my choice. Regardless of who was originally involved, what was said or done by whom, I had a choice of whether to move forward or not, MY choice! Fortunately, I was able to get some great support and even had the opportunity to deal with it directly with my father. We worked through it and both grew from it, even our relationship improved. Even if I couldn't do that, I could still move forward, heal and overcome…

The key was FORGIVENESS for me and for others! I had to forgive MYSELF. Sounds a bit crazy but yes, I needed to forgive myself, just like most of you need to forgive yourself. Our unwillingness to forgive ourselves can even keep us from truly forgiving others. I mention this first because it needs to be done first. Get free yourself, then… move forward with forgiving others. Even if they don't ask, forgive. Forgive freely and often.

Sometimes, forgiveness is more of a process than an event.

Forgiveness is a choice, not a feeling. In time, feelings of joy, peace, relief, freedom and contentment will follow. The freedom not to be like anyone else or expect others to be like me for me to be OK. The freedom to not always prove that I'm right. The security to be around others that are different and not feel the need to be like them (fit in), or to make them be like me by agreement (arguing to win always until they give in or leave). The feeling of security that I'm OK because I'm made wonderful, unique and worthwhile. It didn't mean I was perfect, nor did I have it all figured out (far from it)! It just helped me be in a place where I was secure so I could begin to move forward to where I needed to be. I was able to start letting go of the past so I could embrace the future.

Most, if not all, of us need someone to walk through the process with us. Not because we are weak or bad, but because it is the best way by design. Maybe a mentor, a friend, a family member or a professional; somebody to help us keep things in perspective. Help us keep grounded. Help us not get caught up in false healing by over-inflating our ego. To be more focused on who we are designed to be, and become congruent with that, body, soul and spirit.

So, what is the rest of the story? The journey of healing has been hard at times and painful at others. It has not happened instantly but over time. It is worth every bit of pain, hardship and struggle to become secure, to be the ME I am designed to be. I began to understand my value as a human that was given to me by my Creator. I also began to understand that we all have the same priceless value. Understanding my and others' value freed me to look at others without needing them to accept and always agree with me. The freedom not to always look for approvals from others.

Ed and I came to be great friends as well as colleagues. When I left the company, he was the hardest person to say goodbye to. I finally started to be OK with me. With that, I became OK with him, being him. Are you wounded? If you're human, YES! Can you heal? YES!!

Great, I had started on the road to healing, but what was next? Choices – choices for change. I had begun to feel secure in who I am, so it helped me with a foundation to make choices for change. So, what did that look like for me?

In 1997 I was moving forward with my growing small construction business when I encountered two challenges at once. The first challenge created the second one. I had not figured out how to be in multiple places at one time and cloning was even less developed. Also, I wasn't getting any younger. So, I needed to find workers, preferably qualified workers...

As is currently true, they just weren't to be found. There were a lot of people that wanted to make big bucks but weren't qualified or especially motivated to earn it... (I also had school-aged children at the time...)

So, faced with these challenges, I had to explore options. Partner with others, become more of a General Contractor and get subs, look for other sources... and so on.

My wife suggested something that was not even in my thinking, and at the time sounded a bit insane... (defining moments happen that way quite often!)

She suggested I teach construction... hmm... as she heard there was an opening for a construction teacher at a local high school... Hmm...

Why would I do that? I wasn't qualified and, besides that, I hated school (I was an avid learner but not an academic student). Again, so why would I do that? My faith was challenged as well. How could I do this thing? Like Moses and other characters in the Bible (I'm not in their league but it helps for understanding), I had lots of good excuses. In addition, even with the challenges, it was familiar and 'comfortable'… more comfortable than changing, especially this kind of change (a schoolteacher – really?)!

For various reasons, the schedule lining up with the children, help with the worker problem from others, health insurance and, mostly leading from the Holy Spirit, I acquiesced, somewhat reluctantly. I accepted a new vision of sorts.

I started teaching in the fall of 1998 at the school my wife had mentioned. Getting the job had its own challenges along the way, mostly timing, so I gave up several times, at least in my mind (some call it the death of a vision).

I started teaching from one motivation, trying to help the construction workforce challenges and my schedule to work better for our needs. After a couple of years though, my motivation changed.

I had found a hidden passion to help young people that were much like me as a student. Learners that weren't particularly academic. My vision developed into providing a context for learning for these young people and having a meaningful and positive impact on their lives! God, my Heavenly Father, knew better what I needed and even wanted.

I am now a teacher at heart and will always be. I have a passion to help people, especially young people, discover their Design and Purpose, and become congruent with this. Had I not taken the correct path, who knows? I'm just grateful that, by God's grace, I took the right path, despite myself.

The moral of the story is don't be afraid of challenges, be open to the possibility that there are opportunities for you that are right for you, but you don't understand. Consider that, if God calls you, you are already equipped and/or He will supply what is needed. Also consider that He brings people into our lives to help us, at times, to make the right choices (James 1 and Romans 12:1-2).

Now I found myself in a new role that I wasn't formally prepared for, but where I was committed and determined to do well. I was excited about the new role, and I was making progress in learning about the best way to be the most outstanding teacher... but something was missing. I was making strides forward, but I faced new challenges as well. I even had my life threatened by a student and I was not winning any popularity contests. It wasn't what I expected, nor had I ever experienced it.

I was on a mission to find the missing ingredient. Some would suggest that the missing part was the formal education that I would later receive. I discovered that, although helpful, formal education wasn't the missing ingredient. I remembered a concept that I had learned during a 'Train the Trainer' course I had taken before. The concept was a module called 'Leadership and Group Dynamic'. Leadership was the missing ingredient.

Leadership starts with us learning to lead ourselves... not just any leadership, but servant leadership. I realised I had to treat myself with the same humble approach as I would others, but also in how I lead ME! I had to apply the principles of servant leadership to myself and in my new role as a teacher, as an accidental or default leader. I began applying these principles to myself, but how could I apply them to my students? After all, I was a teacher, not a leader.

As I reflected on this, it began to become clear to me what I was dealing with. I had historically associated titles with positions. Titles such as manager, supervisor, team lead, lead technician, and even ones such as teacher, administrator or parent. In these roles, I/we would think nothing of trying to be a better teacher by reading books, listening to speakers or participating in training. That is well and all, but I was missing something in these cases! What is it, you ask? By default, these roles, and many others, means being a leader! Many, including me, say or think at this point, "I'm not a leader, I'm a teacher!!" I began to refer to this as a 'default leader' because, when I applied leadership in these roles, it was only by default, or accidental.

So! What if I am an accidental leader, so what? I am still a teacher, right? Yes, but I was caught in a frustrating crash and burn as a result. I was working hard to manage all the responsibilities I had been given, including the 'people' drama from my group of students. I struggled with students getting their projects done because I was spending time managing the drama of my students. Ultimately, the projects got done because it is how everyone got a grade, but that still left the grade reports due. I scrambled to get the reports done and usually, it was from bits and pieces of information in my fragmented memory and various notes I had scribbled down or jotted on my tablet, paper or electronically.

To top it all, there was still the thought that other student projects were coming that I really needed to be thinking about already. I was feeling the burn; the burn in my gut, the burn in my mind when I was supposed to be sleeping, the burn of 'crash and burn'.

But wait! I am a good teacher! That happens too. Just by sheer force of personality, I did manage to be a good teacher. I managed to sustain my way through the craziness and survive. But is that the way I wanted to work – survive and just hang on? Did I want my students to get through things, survive the challenges and just have a sigh of relief when finished? I preferred to have a very successful completion and then still have some energy left, or even be inspired and motivated. That is the potential for effective and great leaders. A favourite comment from a fellow trainer and leader, Colin Dunn, is *"You can be a good manager (teacher) without being a leader, but if you want to be a great manager (teacher), you have to be a great leader!"* So, don't let the enemy of great, being good, keep you from being the leader you can be!

So, what is this leadership about? Traditionally, leadership is thought to reside in the boardrooms and executive suites. Sometimes it is born out of a lifestyle that has developed these people into leaders. Sometimes it is born out of having a good idea, working hard to develop it and then becoming financially successful. Sometimes it occurs from sheer force of will and determination. Sometimes, quite accidentally.

The definition I have developed is *"Leadership is the actions and attitudes displayed by one individual while reaching their full potential, that inspires others to reach their full potential as they both pursue a shared vision"*. The key is a well-communicated vision that is shared by one or more people. Management (traditional approach to teaching) is based on authority and control. True leaders, great leaders, rely on being influential and humble role models. Another way to express it is, 'servant leader'. One of the greatest examples is Jesus Christ. Whether you agree with his tenets or not, history has demonstrated and confirmed this fact.

Do you want to be a great leader? Start by being a servant leader with yourself. Another way is to study hard and follow in the footsteps of other great servant leaders. Or seek out help from those that can guide you. Whichever route you decide to get there, apply the principles of leadership in all of your roles, whether they have a title as a leader or not.

As I have become secure in myself as a person, I have become more effective in dealing with life's challenges. I am better at allowing myself to consider opportunities that sometimes even become defining moments. I have learned to approach life as a leader, whether I have a title or not, and especially regarding leading myself.

When you meet Jamal, you cannot help but smile. His energy is high, light and inspiring. Being in the presence of someone highly motivated who has learned the motivational power of teaching others and only wants the best for himself and others, is genuinely refreshing. Jamal's story reflects a man on a mission with a vision that improves lives. His persona is child-like, fuelled with curiosity, fun and excitement, igniting his passion for owning his leadership. It reminds me of the childhood game, Follow the Leader.

Within his chapter, Jamal reveals the characteristics of servant leadership and who you need to become to be successful; he embodies the need to identify your purpose, which provides meaning to your life. It takes a new way of thinking and being. You must value yourself first to add value to others; Jamal does this in spades. Jamal demonstrates the need to question how you can consistently improve every day.

After reading his story, I believe you will ask who you are and who you want to become as a Voice of Strength for today and tomorrow.

Brenda

Jamal Ahmed

"I want my daughter to grow up in a world where every woman, every man and every child enjoys freedom over their personal information anywhere in the world."

Jamal Ahmed

Jamal Ahmed is the CEO of Kazient, a privacy expert and founder of the Privacy Pros, Academy and Privacy Pros. He has a straightforward vision:

> *"I want my daughter to grow up in a world where every woman, every man and every child enjoys freedom over their personal information anywhere in the world."*

The driving force of Jamal's vision is to work on his mission to empower every organisation that processes personal information to ensure they hold it openly and transparently and to be able to empower every organisation to do so with integrity.

○○○

I set up the Privacy Pros Academy to allow businesses to work with us to protect reputations and ensure they're doing things compliantly. Essentially, they must comply to earn trust, cultivate confidence, and ultimately have a more significant impact and success. On the privacy pro side, I realised it doesn't matter how many businesses we work with; we're only a drop in the ocean. We can only start working on the mission to achieve the vision by building a community, a tribe of like-minded professionals worldwide. Coming together will allow us to succeed tremendously in businesses around the GDPR. Once we empower enough businesses to adopt those mass production practices, we will live in a world where my data, your data, and everyone's data, are protected. Then we will enjoy freedom over that personal information wherever we go.

It is crucial to have a reason, a 'why' that allows you to become a trailblazer, a change-maker, and a thought leader. Stepping into leadership and making a difference is crucial to adding meaning to your life.

What was the pivotal moment when you realised that there was more to being a man in the 21st century than following the status quo?

I believe it was probably quite early on in my career. I have always been curious, looking at what happened within situations and how to do it better next time. I'm constantly questioning why things are a certain way. I also ask questions to remind myself of the goal. What is it that we're trying to achieve? One of the challenges I had as a young employee involved speaking to certain managers. They disliked that I asked questions about my tasks. I felt that they just wanted somebody who would follow their instructions without any thought or questions that could improve the situation. It was more of a "Yes, sir. No, sir. Three bags full, sir". It felt robotic; go to work, finish my shift and go home. Living Groundhog Day was not for me.

Whatever job you do, it has to make a difference. It has to be to the best of your ability and must be reviewed and reflected on to improve. The work is always about the customer and the client, and I want to serve them. I am constantly pushing boundaries and asking, "Why are we doing this? What can we do instead?"

It felt like the managers above didn't worry or care about customer service or things that would provide greater customer satisfaction. This frustrated me because I thought anyone could do this mundane job; they didn't need me here to do it. I hadn't invested in my professional education and professional development to do something that anybody could do. I wanted to be adding value. I needed to make sure that everything I'd invested in was getting a return and that I was fulfilling my purpose, helping the world be a better place.

When you question your role this way, you soon discover you have been carrying out tasks without thought. Working like this did nothing to inspire me, but keeping my mouth shut was not an option. There is nothing attractive about being mediocre. I believe we have the potential within us to be outstanding. When adding meaning to your life, you must impact everything you do. We are in this world to make our own lives great and make life better, even if it is for just one other person. That person could be somebody in your own family.

When we do this, we're living life and can be satisfied when we get to the end of it. When you do not achieve this goal, you may start to ask whether it matters or not if we exist. If you do not add value to your life, then I urge you to give meaning to your life by helping and supporting others.

People who choose to write things down, make things happen because it's written down. If you don't put your learning, thoughts and experiences into a book, it's as if it never happened. More importantly, you do not write just anything down. Who will be interested in me telling them

I went to work, I followed the process, I got paid, I paid my taxes and I went home – **nobody**! That is not inspiring.

Everything changes – the tone, mood and voice – the moment you start focusing on how you have thought about making a change. People get inspired when talking about the struggles you've been through, how you overcame them, and what the outcome was for you. When you inspire others to change their thoughts, words and actions, your influence creates a ripple effect, which can then produce incredible results worldwide.

For example, there was someone who came through the practical academies. He had spent his whole life working in the family business, which was an Indian restaurant. He had no formal qualifications, no professional work experience, and he didn't even have a CV. He got fed up working in a restaurant and became an Uber driver. He was still unsatisfied, but then he realised he wanted to change his life. He knew that he had to do something.

The universe bestows us with such synchronicities because that is when he came across us at Kazient. I had previously worked with one of his relatives, and in our first meeting, he showed up with humility, honesty and ambition. He disclosed that he had no legal knowledge, professional experience or technical background. But what he conveyed was a willingness to put in the hard work. He implored, "Can you help me?"

Despite all of his challenges and lack of experience, we managed to support his goal within six months. We empowered him with knowledge, the right mindset and the right attitude, which resulted in him securing a role with a multinational organisation as a Data Protection Manager, despite having no previous experience or qualifications. He succeeded because they saw that he had the right mindset. He is typical of the people who sign up with us, and it illustrates the point that if you can do that, I can do it.

Where did you find the courage to change your mindset, words and actions that strengthened and supported your journey through your transition?

I'd say it takes more courage to have regret. It's scary to think you could have done something and taken action towards what seems too big a challenge. Courage drives you. It focuses on trying your best. If the result is not what you intended, then keep going, find another way, but don't give up. Living with this attitude reaps the rewards and success. When you adopt this mindset, then at the end of the day, you can hold your head up and say, "I had a great day today. I am focused on making a little bit of a difference. I can sleep at night knowing I've contributed to the world you're blessed to experience."

I believe every single day is a blessing; in fact, every single moment is a blessing. When you use this belief to shape your mindset, you understand that you are responsible for ensuring optimum health, so you spend less time worrying about it.

Today, you could argue that we are fortunate to have so much technology around us that we can take it for granted at times. I believe there is no excuse or reason why we shouldn't focus on how we can make each day a better place in the world.

However, we mustn't take all of our blessings for granted. You can strengthen your courage by being grateful. When you express gratitude for everything, it enables you to understand its power. You might say, "I've got all these skills and talents, and I must have been given them for a reason." It's not just to enjoy my life; there is more you can do with my blessings, allowing you to add more value and pay it forward in the world.

What advice would you give someone about adopting a positive and optimistic mindset to change their lives?

You're in charge of your mind; therefore, you control the results. There is much work and evidence on the internet to understand that our brains experience neuroplasticity.

Having this capacity enables you to view whatever you think right now can all change in an instant. When you consciously think differently, you also begin to make those changes. The book *Atomic Habits* by James Clear talks about how we can rewire our brains and adopt practices that will change our behaviours to transform who we are and our identities.

Your perspective on the complexity or simplicity of something is also a choice. How often do you hear someone say, "I can't do that," or "I've always been this way." They are creating a self-fulfilling prophecy instead of creating change. I believe it is a matter of making a decision that favours happiness and fulfilment; therefore, all you need to do is decide who you want to be. After making that choice, you have an identity; and your new actions and habits will support you to achieve your intention.

Positive mindsets develop from understanding that you are responsible and in control of changing your mind your whole life, therefore envisaging the life you want to live. You may also consider your legacy, the impact you want to leave behind. Now think about how you want to show up in the world, and then take steps to be the identity of such a person who will make that happen. Do a straightforward thing towards it every day. Remember, nobody is going to change your world except for you. One step at a time and with consistency, creates a compound effect.

What does it mean for you to be a man who lives his life authentically in a competitive world?

I would say it's more important to focus on competing with yourself every day rather than competing with anyone else. You need to compete with the man/woman in the mirror and make yourself just one per cent better every day.

Whatever you decide to do, as soon as you start showing up as your authentic self, people's perceptions change. In the beginning, you will get a few people supporting you. However, be aware that some will begin to criticise you when they see you enjoying success. Moreover, some will try and dissuade you from continuing, which they hope will hold you back; when they can't do that, they will try and discredit you. Dealing with these challenges and ignoring them needs courage and inner strength. Your success is simply making them feel insecure. It's not anything you're doing and says more about their mental state. My best advice is to forget about everyone else. Ask yourself, "What can I **do** better today than yesterday? How can I **be** better today than I was yesterday?" Your goal is to be the best version of yourself.

It's time to be honest. Changing your mindset is not easy. Think back to your younger days. When you fall off the horse or the bike, you bounce back and get back into the saddle. It's about developing and strengthening your resilience. It's about understanding that mistakes, failures and setbacks are part of success and life's journeys.

What valuable lessons of strength have you learned about yourself?

Being strong means being comfortable knowing that things aren't always where they need to be right now. You may have a long road ahead, and that knowledge allows you to break down the steps into achievable goals with easier wins. When you're doing something actively to take positive steps forward and make changes, whether for yourself, your family, your community or the globe, it is significant and matters to your ability to commit and be persistent. Knowing that you're chipping away at something, even if you don't know what will unfold, is fulfilling and being courageous makes it easier to be true to who you are.

Whatever you do, it is vital to be authentic to your values and beliefs, regardless of everything else that gets in your way. The key is to continue working on implementing what you believe. These beliefs form during your adverse experiences, losses, and challenges. Eventually, you realise that everything you thought once mattered doesn't matter. The only thing that matters is who you are today and how you show up in the world. Your compass points to the things you do each day, such as working on your vision and your missions that align with your values. When you do that every single day, nothing else matters, and that's where true strength comes from knowing you're being true to yourself, living your values and working towards your vision.

It's the commitment to repetition that creates good habits. That consistency of living with authenticity will give you the strength you need to carry on when things get tough. It is the same as going to the gym; eventually, your muscles strengthen and become strong with repeated exercises.

You can also attach your strength to your 'why'. When you have a powerful enough 'why', you find the strength to hold on to it because there's such a gravitational pull toward what you want to achieve. Every single man, woman and child should seek to find and understand their 'why'. Your 'why' identifies your purpose; at this point, everything else falls into place.

What three tips would you give your younger self to help develop the inner strength you need to carry on, day in and day out?

1. Number one is to understand that the art of reflection allows you to review each day, and the best way to do that is to journal every day.

2. The second thing is to surround myself with a positive tribe of mentors. Focus on identifying them and choose carefully. Ensure they reflect your values, research them well and learn everything you can about what makes them successful.

3. Finally, identify who you want to become. List that person's habits and show up as your best future self daily.

Mark Stephen Pooler has these qualities in spades if you want to meet strong, quiet resolve with dignity. A resilient and gentle soul, Mark has overcome many challenges and stands in his power, trusting the man he is today. He writes his chapter with a noble confidence that says, "Look at me and how far I have come," not just for his self-worth but so that others can see it is possible for them too. Mark has learned the power of the inner journey and the introspection it teaches you as you know more about who you are and the value you bring to others and the world. It takes great strength of character to face your truth and do something about the parts that need improving; Mark shows you how.

Storytelling is a vulnerable yet powerful tool. It is no coincidence that Mark finds himself in the world of Public Relations, where he has revealed his story and now enables others to do the same. This quality demonstrates those of an enlightened leader, and Mark arouses the brilliance in others so they can share their story. I call this process Ripples of Brilliance. Sharing beliefs and practices, such as collaboration, making good choices and understanding that it is all right to lose others around you along the way to being the best version of yourself, illustrates that Mark has a Voice of Strength. He fearlessly shares his story so that you, too, can find your inner strength to stand in your authenticity and vulnerability with brilliance.

Brenda

Mark Stephen Pooler

"When you embrace strength
with all your might,
you have the determination
to forge your path
and live life on your terms."
Mark Stephen Pooler

Who have you become?

It is essential to be able to stand with confidence and introduce yourself, saying your name infused with a sense of high self-esteem and self-worth. My name is Mark Stephen Pooler, and I am a global profile builder. I support entrepreneurs with digital media and marketing, and run my own PR agency. Becoming a Voice of Strength has enabled me to become an international bestselling author as well as a web, television and radio host. Everything I have achieved provides me with the opportunity of being an international speaker where I can share my story, vision and message.

What does it mean to be a Voice of Strength?

As you develop, you gain greater insight into who you are, which is vital for success, happiness and well-being. Thinking about the title of this book – *Voices of Strength* – has allowed me to go on that inner journey and consider what it means for me and what insight I can provide to others. The whole point of sharing my story, experiences and learning is to inspire others to look at themselves and consider what changes **they** need to make in their lives and businesses.

Being genuine and authentic makes me a Voice of Strength because I have discovered that in today's modern world, especially in business, not everyone is original. I am always authentic as I lead from the heart, which fuels my personal power and makes me stand out in my field of expertise.

What was the pivotal moment when you realised that there was more to being a man in the 21st century than following the status quo?

I believe I'm not like many other men. I'm a man of values and principles. The majority of men still have the old paradigm of putting importance on status, such as being rich, filling their lives with material things, and believing they have to act a certain way and have certain things before they feel.

When I started my entrepreneurship journey, I was trying to become successful. Like all new entrepreneurs, I was right at the bottom and just starting as a speaker before I had my PR agency. Becoming a public speaker was my intention to share my story. Many successful men and women in business were a lot what I describe as 'higher' than me. They had been in business longer and had seemingly achieved much success, and I thought they were at the top of their game.

I was the new kid on the block, and I think they saw something special in me and felt threatened. I was shocked to experience their fear and ego as they tried to knock me down. Despite being at what I term the bottom of the field, I was unwavering in building some success for myself. Here I was, looking up to these experienced and wise people, yet they continually tried to push me down. I'd had enough of these people and learned to focus on myself instead of them.

This negative experience gave me the determination to succeed. It showed me whom I did not want to be or become. I was going to stand out by being Mark Stephen Pooler.

I was a genuine, authentic person. You have two types of people in business: those who are sincere, and those who are not so natural. Over time I have learned that some people lead with ego. You cannot possibly be authentic when you show in this way. You have to lead from your heart, what you believe in and have a passion for serving others, using your experiences as fuel to drive with purpose. I thank those people who tried to put me down before I achieved success because they were the ones who unleashed my determination to be the person I am in business, being authentic and honest.

I believe in being part of this new-age man, who lives life on his terms, relinquishes ego and embraces authenticity. I think ego should not be a part of business, full stop. I feel being authentic and leading from the heart is vital to happiness and fulfilment. If you're in sales, you should be selling from the heart, coming from a place of service rather than simply looking for what you want to get. It is about empathy and compassion, considering how you can support and help others; developing and using these traits are essential for me and my business.

How does a Voice of Strength know the power of vulnerability?

I have built my whole business by sharing my personal story. So even though I am in a PR business, where I support entrepreneurs with digital media and marketing, sharing my background and story of rising from bullying, severe drug addiction, collapsing and dying from drug use, is critical to who I am. Baring my soul has developed my inner strength. I know my story resonates with so many other entrepreneurs providing them with hope as I have transformed my life. When you share your story, it allows people to connect with you and get to know you. I used to believe vulnerability was weak, but I have learned that it gives you respect because it reveals the honesty and authenticity we all strive to achieve. People can see you are just like them; you're not better than them but perceived as on their level. It is the essence of being human; you're just like them. I think it's vital to find the courage always to share your story. If your story touches one person and creates a change, it is worth it!

How did you find the courage to share your story?

I knew it would be best to dig deep to change from the older person to the brave new person with a stronger mindset. You have to learn to use more positive words to strengthen your journey, knowing that the result is transitional.

I would say it's an ongoing process, and I'm constantly changing and improving myself. Self-development and personal development are essential for change and growth. I embraced personal development at the start of my entrepreneurship journey, which began in network marketing. This sector develops an entrepreneurial spirit and is big on self-development and personal growth.

This opportunity sparked within me the desire to change and improve myself. I started working on my personal development, which has been the whole of the last seven years of this journey. I have constantly focused on myself and my personal development through business coaching, voice coaching, personal growth, life coaching, workshops, seminars, watching YouTube videos, and so on. I am constantly improving myself, and I believe it's a lifelong journey, and I think it's something that never gets done. We can always get better, and we can continually improve.

What does it mean to you to be a man who's living his life authentically in a competitive world?

Firstly, I never look at the competition; I choose not to see rivalry. I hold a strong belief in collaboration over competition. So even if someone in the same industry is selling the same product or service that I'm offering, I will look at ways of collaborating with that person. My superpower is that I am authentic and lead from the heart. I focus on myself and my business, primarily on how I can serve the world. I retract from negativity, particularly envy and jealousy, by understanding emotions and how they propel me forward or hold me back. I am always positive, marvel at other people's achievements and celebrate their success. For these reasons, I always look for collaboration opportunities over the competition.

What are the valuable lessons of strength?

Strength for me would be more vulnerability which sounds like the opposite! But I think significant strength is evident when you can be vulnerable.

Additionally, I think a big part of strength is kindness. Again, in today's business world, some people don't have this trait; if only they could view kindness as strength! You also have to be emotionally strong in your mindset to develop and use the skill of being a good listener.

Furthermore, I would say I have learned that sometimes people can take advantage of your kindness, strength and vulnerabilities. When that happens, you must be firm. Identify and use boundaries that protect you from having people taking advantage of you. I think I'm a lovely person and very kind, but at the same time, you do have to exhibit strength by saying no. You must be able to stand up for yourself so that people don't take advantage of your kindness. When you forget to do this, it diminishes your self-esteem and self-worth.

Another aspect of development is your resilience. When you get back up after each knock, it strengthens your resolve. It allows you to learn and apply the lessons that make you more potent over time. When people kept putting me down, it allowed me to rise again, more significantly and more robustly, because it ignited in me a determination that I could succeed. In turn, it fuels your drive to be a better person than those who only want to see you fail. Resilience enables you to ignore them and provides the laser focus you need to develop and grow.

I also think in life, we make mistakes, and when we keep making the same mistakes, it is because we have not yet learnt the lesson. Again, this is a situation where you further develop resilience to try new things and get out of your comfort zone. All of these circumstances lead to experiences that build your inner strength and strength of character.

What have you learned about yourself through your journey experiences over the last seven years? How do authenticity, honesty and truth create your strength?

The greatest lesson I have discovered is that I am good enough just the way I am. I have toughened myself on the inside and do not let other people's opinions affect me. At the beginning of my journey, I cared too much about others' thoughts. Once you know and acknowledge that you are genuine and authentic, you know that you are good enough, just the way you are. That is my most important and most powerful lesson. The icing on the cake is my integrity and ability, to be honest with myself.

A consequence of this growth and inner strength is losing many people along the way. You also discover that entrepreneurship can be pretty lonely at times. Even though I have a large social following, it can sometimes be very lonely and isolating. It is essential not to fool yourself by the number of followers you have as an entrepreneur because they are followers and not always real connections that become your friends and business associates. I love collaborating with many people in business, but I also protect my space and am conscientious about whom I let into my room. Being protective can also lead to loneliness because entrepreneurship is often a single-minded journey as you pursue your vision with purpose.

When you consider your younger self, what three tips would you give so you can be happy, successful and prosperous?

My three tips for my younger self would be:

1. You are good enough just the way you are. You can spend so much of your life not feeling good enough. So just know that you are good enough, just as you are.

2. Know that you are worthy and deserving of happiness, love, success, health and anything you want.

3. Follow your dreams and passions. My journey has taught me to ignore the many people that tried to hold me back. Stick to what you're good at and find your passion that fuels your goals and dreams. Use your strength and courage to follow your desires and fantasies. Understand that the journey needs endurance and many failures will happen, so use your power to persevere.

The primary human perception of happiness, fulfilment and prosperity is to recognise that you are good enough. Being wealthy in values, positive emotional intelligence and serving others is massive to your whole sense of well-being. If you don't believe that, nothing will leave you feeling that your life has meaning or satisfaction.

As people, we always strive for more because possibilities are limitless, and we are evolving every day through our learning and journey, although you have to know the difference between when to stop and when to keep going. Many people do not realise that the inner journey of self-improvement and personal development is more significant than the outer influences in our lives.

I believe that is why many people continue to do so many courses to gain and improve their knowledge. Instead, if they looked within, they could see they already had all of the answers. They still think they need to know more. There is a spurious fear that others will think we're fake. Education is essential, but it is applying the lessons and taking action that creates the change within us. This lack of feeling 'good enough' drives people to achieve several degrees and leaves them wondering why they can't get a job.

As a Voice of Strength, I must speak out loud, be a beacon of light and lead the way for men to begin their inner journey, so they can find the strength to be resilient, authentic and wise. The wisdom learned along the journey through their experiences must be put to good use in finding and living a life on purpose to provide the meaning we seek. When you embrace this strength with all your might, you have the determination to forge your path and live life on your terms.

*"No one saves us
but ourselves.
No one can and no one may.
We ourselves must walk
the path."*

Buddha

Adam is a charismatic, remarkable man of the world. From the onset, Adam reveals his great storytelling prowess, and his engaging, passionate narrative hooks you, leaving you wanting more. His inheritance is the catalyst for many choices, having lived with exceptional role models in his parents. His strength reveals positive decision-making that puts his needs first and is a great lesson to share. You soon learn of his humanitarian commitment to others and the global accolades bestowed upon him as a direct result of his mother's work.

As you become engrossed in this chapter, many inspirational lessons illustrate a belief in God, the need for spiritual connection and living a life steeped in values and principles. Evidenced in his writing is the essential talent of learning from life, and others, especially leaders, infusing the richness of these lessons into your life, and relating the storytelling so audiences can also blend new ideas with their schemas creating new notions. It takes great courage, inner strength and resilience to stand against the resistors, to walk the road less travelled and forge your path, and Adam explains why passion and purpose lead to ultimate happiness and fulfilment.

Brenda

Adam Greenwell

*"Keep your eyes
on your vision."*
             Adam Greenwell

When the Politics of a Family
Are the Politics of a City and a Nation

Following the passing of both of my parents – my father in 2016 and my mother in 2020 – my concepts of family, legacy and starting my own family came to the fore even though I was well into middle age. Reflecting on my choices as a young man, I came to use the analogy of Jack and the Beanstalk as one who had swapped the 'cow' (career, prestige) for the 'magic beans' (an unguaranteed promise of greater horizons). At the same time, like young Jack, I have an inheritance that enables me to take on giants, obtain riches and reclaim what has been stolen.

I learned in the 21st century that things leading up to that point had prepared me, such as the music/writing interests that I developed as a younger man.

My mother, who survived 35 years as a kidney transplant recipient when she passed, left a legacy called 'Watering the Fields of Humanity' – a global cooperation uniting people of goodwill, integrating the core technologies needed and finding the means of financial support needed. I have continued her legacy and commitment as can be seen from this quote from the University of Embu in Kenya, appointing me as the Chair of the University Advisory Board earlier this year:

The University of Embu commends you for your ongoing strong commitment to the overall global vision of Watering the Fields of Humanity worldwide, held by your late mother, Professor Elizabeth Greenwell (Energime University). That work, prior to and following her passing, led you to establish strong ties, and written agreements, with the Kenya National Commission for UNESCO (KNATCOM) and the University of Embu.

In your own right, you have demonstrated for nearly three decades how the production of music enhances education and community spirit. Your work, archived by the Mayor of Palmerston North, New Zealand, your former home, was acknowledged by heads of state and global public figures.

Without my father, without his name, choices and character, the circumstances both my mother and I found ourselves in – both positive and negative – would not have happened. My father remains my father, for better or worse, and I work through that journey of the forces that shape me in one of my published articles, 'A Greenwell in New Zealand' (*World Growth Forums Magazine*).

Shortly after my parents separated, I would visit my father in the hotel in Palmerston North where he was staying and we would then go to a local cafe or for a walk. One afternoon, as a 16-year-old schoolboy, I was met by the well-dressed owner of the hotel. "I know your father," he said. "I know your father very well. <u>Ken's with us now</u>. If you want to see your father, ask for me."

I was faced with two heavy challenges growing up.

Firstly, I had to pinpoint who belonged to a Mafia-like cabal called the KWUN ("Ken's With Us Now"). Taking the phrase "Ken's With Us Now" by the said wealthy local businessman, it became something of a mission and an exercise of recovery: to find out the motives of an obviously well-connected group of wealthy locals and their desired effect on me and my loved ones. I needed to know who the "Us" in KWUN were, and what they wanted with my family.

Secondly, there was a rising sense of hurt and resentment over how and why my father left me in that predicament.

Seeing all this as an unnecessary burden when life is too short, I made a prudent decision to use my mother's maiden name of Coyle and claim my Irish heritage at the same time. I would also leave New Zealand after finishing my degree. I refused to be damaged by a sneering mob in a country that was tiny in the overall scheme of things. By dispensing with the Greenwell name and getting out of New Zealand, I would be free of two very heavy loads that came with the KWUN.

My academic career was well set. I was planning visits overseas and seeing clarity and lightness in the road ahead. My father, whom I took to be a rational man, would live with my decision. But his reaction shocked me. He said he was "deeply hurt". My father rarely admitted to being bothered about anything, except injustices that caused human suffering everywhere. I loved him especially for his social concern, which I thought would make him more philosophical about my choices.

Whilst I had well and truly washed my hands of the KWUN, I sadly became estranged from my father, even though I did not love him any less. Naturally, I looked up to ask God what He was doing, and what I was supposed to be doing, thus ending up with a rich spiritual life in the process.

My faith, which fluctuated over the years, solidified once I thought less about religion and more about spirituality. To that end, the adage "whoever sings, prays twice" turned out to be accurate as I pursued music, not with a career in mind, but as a means of being honest in expressing myself and thus becoming a better person. Of course, as a younger man, I was concerned about how I appeared, how my goals may have looked like dreams and, of course, returning to an academic career once the projects were complete. Returning to my faith and a sense of calling about what I was doing gave me a sense of a vocation. With that vocation comes the belief in a sense of completion, or things making complete sense in the final analysis.

I am reminded of my private conversation with a very successful businessman cited as a "key influencer and stakeholder". When I was sharing my thoughts with him, he replied, "I'll stop you there. That would be beautiful, but it won't work. Too many tools and a*******s". For whatever reason, I noticed that the people who warned me about coming up against resistance were the very people pushing back. To remain authentic in a competitive world, I recall the words of my father: "Figure out the mind game."

Many people get frustrated or despondent at life's injustices, yet working out the 'mind game' of the resistor actually leads to positivity, a focus on solutions and pleasing results. Being authentic means that the effects of hostility and discouragement, though upsetting, do not define who we are and what we stand for. Our values, principles and objectives should remain intact, no matter what.

If I believe that my cause is just and right, I will stay the course with the courage of my convictions. Perhaps the biggest price I have paid is forgoing a wife and family due to the emotional and financial costs of remaining on track. Yet great friends, confidants and companions in the journey have gathered around me after my long trek through a desert of loneliness and loss.

Another lesson of strength is my desire to tell the definitive story of Sir Roger Douglas, a polarising yet historic figure cited as "New Zealand's best-ever finance minister" and "the author of the most successful economic reform of the 20ᵗʰ century".

After hearing Sir Roger informally speak in a small group at a social gathering in 1986, I became convinced over time that his economic legacy is not about neoliberalism (policies advocating self-interest and the increase of poverty and unemployment), as has been widely written by academics and journalists for nearly forty years. Sir Roger Douglas has always been about the best delivery of economic gain and social welfare to the "people at the back of the line". Since presenting my story publicly, I have enjoyed the robust debate melded with new perspectives from former opponents of his policies. That is reflected in another of my published articles, 'Sir Roger Douglas: Limited Public Image and the Punk Rock Star Economy' (*i-Transform Magazine*).

Sir Roger's economic reforms were lauded by colleagues of the late former Czech president and human rights champion, Václav Havel. The Czech Republic (previously Czechoslovakia) had lived under both Fascism and Communism for decades, and could thus relate to the liberating aspects of Sir Roger's policies.

I am reconciling this country's history with my own. Reconciling a reforming government at the time that acted as an extended 'family' to me when my parents divorced and my other relatives were across the miles in the UK and Ireland. Reconciling the dreams of my parents and me when we emigrated to New Zealand from the UK as a small family. Both of my parents are gone, with some of those dreams realised. I am reconciling the memories of the fourth Labour Government as a secular, this-worldly equivalent of the Catholic Church and Christian faith that I was still coming to terms with.

My mother once commented on my interest in and admitted great affection for John Lennon and David Lange (former Prime Minister of New Zealand, 1984-89). It stood to reason, as they were both charismatic public figures. Mum then pointed out that both men reminded me of my father and I was learning more about my father by studying them. Many of the fourth Labour Government were the same age as the Beatles, grew up in the 1960s, and offered the same promise of new and exciting ways to look at the world.

John Lennon's murder devastated me as a boy just entering my teens. The great sadness that consumed me and continued to affect me always intrigued me. Havel's book *Letters to Olga*, written to his wife from his prison cell, pinpointed what I was feeling, what he was feeling and what many were feeling: *"I do not believe that certain values and ideals of the 1960s have been discredited as empty illusions and mistakes, though it is a history of repressions, murders, stupidities, wars, and violence, it is at the same time a history of magnificent dreams, longings, and ideals."*

At Massey University, I later appealed for John Lennon to be awarded a posthumous honorary doctorate – one practical way of connecting the ivory towers of academia with the real world. The conversation, helped by my time on the University Council, did lead to the broadening of criteria for honorary doctorates. That led to Sir Peter Jackson getting one, and later going on to make the *Get Back* series about the Beatles and organise John Lennon's virtual duet for Sir Paul McCartney's 80th birthday.

Three tips to my younger self to develop inner strength

1. **Believe** in yourself.

2. **Trust** in God.

3. Keep your eyes on your **Vision**.

My passion and purpose are about the community, being positive, and protecting freedom and welfare.

"Don't wait for extraordinary opportunities. Seize common occasions and make them great. Weak men wait for opportunities; strong men make them."

Orison Swett Marden

Often as humans, we fail to trust others. Stories, experiences and belief systems impact our inner story, sometimes lessening our strength, resilience and courage. When you read Sam Dossa's story, you will soon learn the power of vulnerability revealed at the beginning of his chapter and woven throughout. Sam's honest, heart-wrenching tale will grab you and awaken the realisation of being human, not just a man.

Like all stories filled with adversity and challenge, it is uplifting to see the heroes rise when they fail, and rise perhaps not once or twice, but many times. Your inner strength intensifies, and the lessons learned fuel your next step. Sam's transformation from a man who believed that men should have their s**t together, to one that embraces the need to cry, releasing negative energy and promoting healing, epitomises the values intertwined in *Voices of Strength*. Unafraid and passionate, he is motivated to share his story, the mightiness of embodying emotional intelligence, using his wisdom, and knowing that he is a man and it's OK to cry.

Brenda

Sam Dossa

*"We are born to win
but conditioned to FAIL!"*
                    Sam Dossa

Man Enough To Know

I was crying.

But no one must see me cry; I am a man!

I was in a large four-bedroom, detached house in one of the posh residential areas of London. I was sat in a corner in the well-decorated living room, and I felt at loss – loss of my life, my children and my marriage. The house was full of valuable material objects, yet I felt that I owned nothing.

This was back in 2013.

My wife had just walked out with my three young daughters to be with another man.

I wasn't even sure that mourning the death of my marriage was a fair thing to do. We had been drifting apart for years. Although we stayed under the same roof, our home life was robotic. We each worked and continued living in our own emotional bubbles. We hardly spoke to each other. If we ever did, it did not sound like 'speaking'. It was shouting, accusing, blaming, falling out and screaming, followed by becoming silent for days. It was toxic.

I had worked around the clock for 17 years, where I had gone to work, come home and then taken over responsibility for our kids. There was not a chance to catch my breath, until a few years ago, when I reconnected with my faith and started my regular morning meditative prayers. About seven years before my wife left, I had taken one step back and had re-evaluated myself, to find out that in the whole rat race of getting better pay, a bigger house, lavish holidays and secure futures for my kids, I had abandoned one thing that was closest to my heart – **my faith**.

I re-connected.

I started my regular prayers and felt a shift in my demeanour and my patience with my life situation. I felt guided and protected.

It hurt to look back and see that my marriage was failing. I wasn't too sure if this was it or if I should continue to try and revive it. I did the latter. I continued to try and hold the fort on my own. My children were my refuge. As long as I saw that I was doing the right thing for them, I was OK doing everything I was expected to do, and more.

And I always smiled.

Our social contacts and friends would tell us about how they thought that we were an ideal couple. We had all our stuff planned and working for us – money, work, children, the future.

No one could possibly see or know about the coercive control, manipulation and financial abuse I was facing.

During this time, I ardently believed that a man must always have all his s**t together. And that's also what I learned while growing up, that a man is a strong being and has to stay strong and NOT be emotional. I stuck to this. I never let anyone see my fears and my tears. If I had to, I cried while in the shower or in the rain. My emotions did not make sense to me.

But no one must see me cry; I am a man!

Of course, lots of effort, attention and energy went into this. And to no use, really! I only spiralled downwards.

For this marriage, I had left behind my birthplace, my family, and my familiar work and social culture. I had taken a big leap while relocating from Pakistan to the UK, and I was hopeful. I achieved a lot in terms of work, and progressed academically and financially. This marriage also gave me my most valued assets – my three beautiful daughters. But it also took away from me *my* values. I often say now that I had lived by other people's values, not mine, and I mean everyone else's but mine.

This commitment also cost me to miss my mum's funeral, as my twin daughters had just been born and I had to be there for them and their mother. My mum's death shook me to the core. She had committed suicide. None of my siblings knew what had happened. We were left double-guessing what we knew and doubting everyone, yet feeling extremely ashamed and guilty that our mum couldn't speak to us. I wanted to scream and cry. I hid and cried.

But no one must see me cry; I am a man!

It was after this mental and emotional turmoil, that I had to be referred to a counsellor. During these sessions, I not only reconciled with myself and became open to growth, I also opened up to a dark secret that I had kept hidden all these years.

At the age of 12, I was molested by a grown man. I had never spoken about this to anyone at all. This secret caused me frustration and anger, and damage to my perception of the world and a man's place in it. While growing up, I was always told to "man up" and I thought until this point that by having not shared this with anyone, I had been a strong man. Inside, I had been crumbling at its memory every single time it came to me.

I gradually got better.

During this time, I discovered that it is possible to liberate yourself from pain. It is OK to acknowledge, accept and understand your emotions. I also learnt that being a man should not feel like being in jail. At the end of the day, a man is as human as anyone else. When we condition men to believe that they have to act in a certain manner, they become restricted; not just their thoughts, but their growth is stunted too.

Who says it's not OK for a man to cry?

Who says that a man must have ALL the answers to all questions?

Who made the rule that macho is the only way forward?

What scripture tells you that a man is only masculine energy?

I started to see how this conditioning had destroyed and disrupted many lives, and how these barriers needed to be broken.

My mantra that I devised is "We are born to win but conditioned to fail".

Inspired by my own growth and liberation, I qualified as a counsellor myself. Now, I wanted to help others. I also took a course in adult teaching, so I was able to understand and take a holistic approach, while also looking to create varied opportunities for myself. I went on to become a qualified coach. I now knew that life was way bigger and better than what I had comprehended it to be. I had been following a tunnel vision, which was not even my own. I was ready for change. I was ready for growth.

After all these changes, I believed that I was now ready to deal with anything that life may throw at me.

And here I was now… sat in a corner of a huge house, not knowing how to feel about this all…

I had failed. I had failed my mum, my father, my siblings, my children, and myself.

I was broken.

Predominantly, it was my kids' loss that I could not bear. They were a big part of my life and I felt empty now.

Once again, **my faith** came to my rescue.

In this place, I understood that we can never control what's happening around us. The only thing we have control over is our choice of response towards that situation. During my developmental year, I had studied Emotional Intelligence. It was now time to put that to practice, which I did.

I had done enough work on myself by now to understand that it is mindset that can make you win or lose. Now I knew that I did not have to follow the status quo to establish myself as a man, a coach, a leader. I was just fine the way I was. I had to further develop my authentic self and move forward.

That evening, I cried. I didn't care if people saw me. I didn't care if they judged me.

I am a man and it's OK to cry.

From this point onwards, it was as if I was put on a path that was to unravel ahead of me. I did not know what it was and where I was headed, but I believed this to be my path.

There were numerous things that I learnt about myself during this time.

To Live in the Moment

I can only live the moment I am in.

It was no use lamenting over the past or stressing about the future. None of them has their true existence. Both past and future borrow energy from the moment I am in, to look real. One fuses this energy into them while feeling sorry about the past or anxious about the future. All fears are caused by thinking of the future, and all bitterness by thinking too much of the past.

The more you are able to live in the now, the lesser you suffer.

To Be Alive and Healthy

I must stay healthy to have a fulfilling life.

I went on a journey to make myself healthier, internally and externally. I focused on practices that enhanced my good health, physically, mentally and emotionally, especially emotionally. I understood that staying at peace with yourself is the biggest blessing of all. I dug deep into Emotional Intelligence and was liberated to find out that my emotions have nothing to do with my surroundings, only my personal interpretation of what they meant.

To Be Grateful

Gratitude turns what we have into enough.

I had my faith. I had my children. I had my health. I had the blessings of my mum and her fond memories. I had hope of a better future and belief that "This too shall pass…"

I decided to surrender to everything that was. To accept my internal conditions when I struggled to accept the external ones. I decided to abide in the state of acceptance and create no further negativity. I decided to be grateful for all that was and stay positive.

I adopted an attitude of "What is meant to be, will be". This, in return, created greater resilience in my persona and gave me the courage to continue to build myself without the fear of judgement from others or failure of my efforts.

To Surround Myself With Positive People

Do not expect positive changes in your life if you surround yourself with negative people. I learnt this in my transformational times.

I started joining circles that uplifted my spirit, made me happier and cheered me on in my journey.

My layers came off as if an onion were being peeled.

I invested in my personal and professional development further and started to talk about my journey. My story and my talks were received well. I became known for how I had beaten adversities, changed myself to be a happier and healthier person, and carried on having a fulfilling life. I had championed the art of making decisions. And this turned out to be the key ingredient to creating a purpose-driven life.

Making decisions is an important part of our lives. We are always making decisions – sometimes actively, sometimes passively. When we are indecisive and choose not to make a decision, we have already chosen the alternative. Our life is a series of reflections on the decisions or indecisions that we make. If we want to change something actively, we will have to decide to change what we can.

I discovered that I was not the only one who had felt threatened and restricted by the so-called social restrictions. Many men have experienced and are experiencing this and sometimes fail to express themselves due to fear of judgement by their surroundings. Inspired by how we can touch each other's life and create a positive change, I started a men's group called MenTell Health®, which runs support groups and projects for the betterment of men's mental health.

I have gone on to win numerous awards for my services.

My true reward is knowing that I am living by my own values now. My true reward is that I can now stand in front of a crowd and help them to uncondition their conditioned minds. True blessing is to see the light being passed on; the flame being shared.

Nobody chooses pain. We stay in the state of mind that causes it because our conditioned mind is running it. We have to unlearn many things to learn the truth about ourselves. And that is OK too.

If I was given a chance to speak to my younger self, I would only challenge it with this: "Be a man enough to know YOUR truth."

Today, I am proud that while helping others to do so, I am that Man.

"We gain strength, courage and confidence by each experience in which we really stop to look fear in the face... we must do that which we think we cannot."

Eleanor Roosevelt

Simon Ong's energy precedes him when he walks into a room. It is an energy fuelled by positive choices, action and a self-empowering belief system. You know that such a person has immersed themselves into a life of learning, not just from books and others, but the powerful lessons about oneself from the situations, environment and poor choices you make along the way. When you embark on an inner journey, your voice rises as you strengthen your resilience, understanding and love of life. From his chapter, it is evident that Simon believes everything is energy and, as such, is the catalyst for all he embraces.

As you continue to read Simon's words of wisdom, you realise that his power lies in his honesty and intention to know and understand himself. Understanding the concept of success and what it means for you enables you to create an environment where you cannot fail to succeed. The great insights revealed will spark your curiosity to discover more about yourself and establish where your energy rises and where it falls. With this knowledge, you can apply it to write your beliefs as the author of your story. You can achieve everything you want with courage by utilising the energy within. Enjoy the enlightened words that follow.

Brenda

Simon Alexander Ong

"Vulnerability makes you human, and that's what the world needs."
Simon Alexander Ong

Voices of Strength **is a book about men forging their path in the 21ˢᵗ century. They're going against the grain and refusing to follow. When did you realise that you were such a man and didn't want to be the same as all other men?**

I think the forging of my path began during the global financial crisis of 2008. Up until then, I had followed the traditional route that most people follow: going to school, achieving my grades, leading on to a respected university and getting a job in the corporate world. But the financial crisis made me question what I was doing. Was I doing something that I enjoyed? Was I doing something that made me happy? And the answer was no.

I began to observe that many of us are exhausted, not because we are physically doing too much, but because we are not giving ourselves time to do all the other things we enjoy. Secondly, I felt that we are all running someone else's race. I realised this way of life wasn't for me, and so I started asking myself questions such as, "What does success mean to me?" and "What sort of impact do I want to have in the world?"

These questions led me to my most significant challenge in the following years, when I decided to own my life and own my future. Taking control of my life was essential to building a life around those answers. And, like all great answers, they lead us on to more thought-provoking questions. This situation opened up a new path towards creating and building my future where I wanted to be, and that is when the journey I am now on began.

"You can't live your best life or produce your greatest work if you don't like what you do."

What I realised at that point, and since then, is that the longest journey we make as humans is the few inches from our head to our heart. Admittedly, it is not an easy journey because it will be full of challenges, setbacks and obstacles, but it will be the most fulfilling and exciting. We must avoid the trap that Bronnie Ware speaks about in her thought-provoking book, *The Top Five Regrets of the Dying*. Bronnie worked for many years in palliative care and decided to write about the regrets that many of her patients had at the end of their life. The top regret was that people wished they lived a life more true to themselves than others. If we heed those words from people who have lived their life already, we can focus our energy on genuinely living and building the talents, skills and gifts given to us at birth.

How did you find the courage that changed your mindset and supported your journey through a transition period?

It has been brought to my awareness that the work of American Dr David Hawkins, internationally renowned spiritual teacher, psychiatrist, physician, researcher, lecturer and developer of the *Map of Consciousness*, illustrates that courage is the energy that transforms our lives. It is the starting point of taking control and using it to live the life we choose.

I, too, think that the journey of transformation begins with courage. We can mistakenly think we need confidence, but courage comes before confidence. When you do something that you've not done before, it builds your confidence. For me, courage started to come when I shifted my environment.

Sometimes I am asked, "What is the fastest way to succeed in any area of our life, career or business?"

Simply put, it is to design an environment around you that makes it impossible not to succeed. So I started spending time outside of work, and on the weekends I would seek out environments I could immerse myself in for inspiration. I joined Mastermind groups. I hired mentors and coaches. I changed the books I was reading, and I would watch TED Talks. I started to watch and consume anything that would elevate my energetic state. Once you operate from a higher energetic state, you discover your courage. You begin to find the courage required to take those small steps forward. And that's all you need at the beginning; you have to take that first step.

Once you take that first step, you build your confidence, and then you take another step, and another step. Before long, you build momentum, which I like to call 'a feeling of going places'; nothing can make you feel quite as energised as that feeling of momentum. Because once you begin to achieve your goals and they are behind you, the newfound confidence ignites bigger and bolder thinking within your mind. You begin to ask yourself, "What else can I achieve? What else can I explore?" The realms of possibility are endless, and that's when excitement kicks in.

You are on a journey of continuous improvement, which is the catalyst that enables you to connect with who you are, your passion and your purpose. When you find yourself in that place, you can speak, and speak your truth. You finally find your voice, and it sparks the mission allowing you to take action relating to your purpose, giving meaning to your work and life.

What does it mean to be a man living life authentically in a competitive world?

I have a different perspective. Rather than focus on being a man, I prefer to consider what it means to be a human, and I resonate more with speaking about that. When I think about what it means to be human, I perceive it as leadership, beginning with leading ourselves first. Being human means understanding who we are, appreciating we are a miracle and bringing value to the world.

Our value as a human is determined by how much more we have given to the world than we have taken from it.

To touch on our legacy virtues, we must know ourselves; true wisdom knows you first, so we must learn to balance it. I am more interested in the idea of what it means to be human, because we all have masculine and feminine energies, so to live as a human is to express our potential and connect with others. We must learn to connect to ourselves at a deeper level and embrace those masculine or feminine qualities. The greatest gift we can give others is not material wealth, but it is the space for feeling appreciated, trusted and heard. That is the greatest gift we can give others, which requires us to connect with them from our human selves.

What it means to be human is to appreciate life and the fact that you are a miracle. Many people wish they would win the national lottery, yet we have already won the most incredible lottery ticket; the miracle of life! The question is, what will you do with your winning ticket?

I also question what my purpose on earth is. You're not going to wake up one morning and know what that purpose will be for the rest of your life. But it begins with asking yourself, "What makes me curious? What does my energy speak?" Listen to those whispers inside of you. Doing this makes you more closely aligned with your true self.

Consider how you can bring value into the world. How can you share your gifts, talents and skills with the world so that everyone can benefit from your presence?

Maya Angelou said,

> *"People will forget what you said,*
> *people will forget what you did,*
> *but people will never forget how you made them feel."*

When you align with your purpose, it always puts others at the heart of everything you do. Servant leaders are about improving other people's lives, significantly changing their energy state. So making them feel happier and inspired to take action adds meaning to your life and brings you joy. I'm sure you have noticed the feedback from people when you've spoken to them; their faces light up, they're smiling and they often say, "Thank you, I feel better now." And the beauty is that you might not have said much to them. A simple smile and greeting can be enough to change a person's life, and it costs nothing.

Outstanding leadership takes vulnerability. I connect with that notion of vulnerability. Because I've learned that the gateway to connection is vulnerability, but it does not make you less of a leader. Vulnerability makes you human, and that's what the world needs. The world needs more humanness because we want to feel connected to the people who lead us. We want to connect to those above us. After all, they are likelier to show up as the best version of themselves.

What valuable lessons of strength have you learned about yourself on your journey so far?

I think the most significant insight I've had about strength is that we are equipped with the wisdom and strength to come back stronger in our darkest, most challenging times. We never know how strong we are until we face obstacles that we never imagined we would ever meet. Some of my darkest moments include: losing my mum at the age of 17 to a tragic accident, failing my second year at university, being made redundant 14 months into my first job at a company called Lehman Brothers due to the financial crisis, and facing the possibility of going back to employment after my first year and a half in entrepreneurship. All these moments have shaped me, but I think those moments are essential to show you how strong and capable you are of achieving beyond your perceived potential. Without adversity, how would you know how strong you are?

In adversity and the darkness, the stars shine. Your energy needs to embrace and own those stories and give thanks for them. The flicker of light gives hope, enabling you to rise like a phoenix.

What three tips or advice would you give to the younger Simon?

My first piece of advice to the younger Simon would be to value your opinion rather than those of others, because you have wisdom inside of you and to access it, you must make space for it to be heard. It is why silence is far from empty; it is full of the insights that you seek, if you are willing to embrace more stillness in your routine.

The second piece of advice would be to focus your energy on being better than who you were yesterday, not on being better than others. Because if you focus your energy on being better than others, it is a waste. You will never win because there will always be someone better than you at something.

The third bit of advice would be getting to know you. Get to know who you are, what you stand for, what you believe in, and your purpose. Because once you understand who you are and what is important to you, you will awaken the greatest source of energy that we as humans possess.

Meet the
Voices of Strength

Douglas Vermeeren

Douglas Vermeeren is considered one of the top leaders in personal development and achievement psychology. He is considered by many to be the modern-day Napoleon Hill for his extensive research into the lives and psychology of more than 400 of the world's top achievers.

In addition, Douglas is the creator of 'Learn to Sell or Die' which helps you unlock sales tools and strategies for today's marketplace. He is a also multi-talented actor, stuntman, director and producer.

Douglas is the author of three books in the Guerrilla marketing series and one in the Dummies book series as well as being the creator of the personal development films *The Opus, The Gratitude Experiment* and *The Treasure Map. Enterprise Magazine* calls him Canada's Tony Robbins! Douglas is the regular featured achievement expert on FOX, FOX Business, CNN, ABC, NBC, CTV, CBC and others.

Twitter: @Vermeerendoug
Instagram: DouglasVermeeren
TikTok: DouglasVermeerenactor

Dexter Moscow

As a presentation skills coach and practitioner in **Positive Intelligence**, Dexter helps his clients create business-winning sales presentations, pitches and conversations, giving them the confidence to realise their full potential both personally and professionally.

From a career in advertising, property and TV, he has a unique style of coaching based on his work in front of the camera for QVC's The Shopping Channel where he sold millions of pounds worth of products for major brands, and behind the camera taught others to do the same.

In an age of Zoom and online video communication, these same processes apply.

www.audiencedynamics.co.uk
www.linkedin.com/in/dextermoscow
www.facebook.com/Dexmoscow
Instagram: dexter.moscow

Shareef Amin

Shareef Amin is a British veteran, humanitarian and author. He served in Afghanistan for nine years which sparked his humanitarian drive to help others in need.

After leaving the army, Shareef ventured into the field of security and protection, putting his skills to good use. During this time, he continued to work on himself as he planned a bright future.

When the Ukraine war broke out and Volodymyr Zelenskyy put out the call for help, Shareef did not hesitate to answer by researching how he could be of service. Within a short time, he found himself in Ukraine, providing humanitarian aid before venturing into medical and army training. On one mission, he was severely injured before being flown back to the UK two months after being wounded in action. After a series of operations, Shareef is planning to return to Ukraine to support on a humanitarian level.

Dennis Pitocco

Dennis is the Founder and Chief ReImaginator of 360° Nation, encompassing a wide range of multimedia enterprises, including BizCatalyst 360°, the award-winning global media digest; 360° Nation Studios; and GoodWorks 360°.

Collaborating with his Chief Inspiration Officer, Ali, their mission is to rediscover humanity at its best, influencing it every step of the way. Together, they do their very best to figure out what the world is trying to be – then using all their resources to help it to be better every day in every way. They embrace the notion that it's not about me or you; it's about caring for the people we serve. And they believe it's about showing up, being present and intentionally giving our invaluable gifts of time, talent and treasure "for good" vs. for profit.

www.linkedin.com/in/dennisjpitocco
Twitter: @bizmasterglobal

Matt Evans

Where to start...

I have made a tonne of mistakes and even more bad choices, but I believe that every single one of them has made me stronger. I've been on the canvas more times that Rocky Balboa, but I have come back stronger every time.

When you feel that you have hit rock bottom, that feeing of rising again is actually quite exhilarating. Why? Because when you have been that low, the only way is up and up and up!

I am a family man and I love my girlfriend and children more than anything. I want them to be proud of me.

I have huge aspirations for the next 12 to 15 years of my life and NOTHING will stop me achieving my goals.

www.get-back-up.co.uk
www.linkedin.com/in/matt-evans-89650232

Satwinder Sagoo

A certified Menopause Coach, Satwinder Sagoo helps women who can't have, or won't have, HRT to find their own positive power. He shows women the good within themselves and changes their perspective on menopause, energising them to see the positives of the menopause journey.

He also supports relationships during menopause, which tend to often feel the heat of women's mid-life transition.

As a bestselling author, having been featured in multiple global articles, won awards and made appearances on TV, radio and podcasts, Satwinder's energy is boundless, and his passion for his business is incredible and heartwarming.

He is on a mission to help men and women understand each other and work as a team to become an unstoppable force against the challenges of menopause.

www.linkedin.com/in/sat-the-menopause-man-sagoo-b4a19450

Prof. Dr Jagdish Khatri

Prof. Khatri is an academician, corporate trainer, author, keynote speaker, visiting professor and mentor. He served as Director and Chair-Holder of UNESCO Network Chair, Mandsaur University, India; Director of an MBA College, Sanskaar College of Management, Allahabad, India; President of Allahabad Management Association; Mentor at International House of Speakers; and Trainer with The Knowledge Academy in the UK.

He has conducted thousands of hours of training, and his book, *Discover Your S.E.L.F.*, is translated into eight languages. He has received countless awards, including Global Goodwill Ambassador, and Professor of Excellence by the International Institute of Influencers.

Jagdish is an international speaker, and has presented academic papers worldwide which have been translated and published globally. As a rare mark of respect, 'Jagdish Khatri's Students Forum' was established in his honour by students at Allahabad, India in 2006.

www.linkedin.com/in/jagdishkhatrileadership

George Greig

George Greig is a Highland Scot, born and raised in rural Aberdeenshire. After undertaking a stone masonry apprenticeship, he decided to join the army at the tender age of 16. He attended the Army Apprenticeship College in Harrogate, North Yorkshire, a decision that changed his life.

After graduating as a Radio Telegraphist in the Royal Signals, he spent the next 24 years in what he described as "army barmy" mode, totally focused on securing each position at the earliest opportunity.

Today, George is the CEO of his own IT solutions and services business, getITright Ltd, and lives in Wiltshire.

He is passionate about words and writing. As well as writing a children's book and poetry, he is the author of *Untapped Potential: Born in Scotland, Found in the Royal Signals*.

www.linkedin.com/in/georgegreig
Twitter: @GeorgeG354

Colin Tansley

Colin Tansley is a former soldier and police officer.

As a young man, Colin trained as an Army Apprentice for two years before being deployed in the UK and overseas, including a tour in Northern Ireland in the late seventies.

Subsequently joining the police, he enjoyed roles in uniform, plain clothes, child protection, training and management. During those times, he witnessed first-hand the effects of rioting in the early eighties, the miners' strike of 1984, child abuse and fighting crime at the 'sharp end'.

He is the author of *Mastering the Wolf*, his memoir detailing his time in the police force.

A father, stepfather and grandfather, Colin's passion to investigate, risk-manage, protect vulnerable businesses and push back against unfairness is a testament to the work he does now with his company, Intelect.

www.linkedin.com/in/colintansleyintelect
Twitter: @intelect_group

Matt Mo CVO

Born in Germany, Matt set out to explore the world in 1990, when his mum discovered the UAE and took over a company in Dubai. At a time when most people couldn't even locate Dubai on a map...

The years after high school took Matt on an extremely successful and versatile career path in the hotel industry, during which he lived and worked in more than 30 different countries, while staying connected and committed to his home – the UAE. Since 2005, Matt has been a Business and Growth Coach with a track record of having coached thousands of people around the world.

Matt is constantly touring across the Middle East, making his content available via his Coaching and Mentorship programs. He also delivers keynotes at conferences and participates in panel discussions.

Matt is on a mission to give YOU **Motivation** to achieve, **Mindset** to believe and **Income** to breathe.

www.linkedin.com/in/mattmocvo
Twitter: @mattmocvo

Eric Francis Manu

Eric Francis Manu, FRSA, is an executive coach, TEDx speaker, etiquette principal, consultant lecturer and entrepreneur. A graduate of Cambridge University, he is a Member of the Association for Coaching® (AC), and is currently studying at Harvard Business School. In 2018, Eric was recognised for his contribution to the hospitality/ etiquette industry, winning the Global Commonwealth Hospitality category at The Big Ben Awards at the Houses of Parliament. He was the first ever black and ethnic minority winner of this prestigious award.

Eric features in various media outlets, and has written articles in *Professional Wealth Management* and the *Financial Times*. He speaks on various platforms worldwide. He brings experiences and tools into the workplace by connecting people to the heart and mission of the organisation through laughter and discipline, while celebrating individual achievements.

"Change Yourself, Change One Person, Change The World".

www.linkedin.com/in/ericfrancismanu
Twitter: @efmanu

Dr Kevin Ward

Kevin Ward is known as #WKWPeopleBuilder and #WisdomSeeker who uses his ability with people to help them find their potential by becoming #ServantLeaders, starting with themselves!

Using his experience as a military leader, organising, planning, coordinating and executing training exercises, Kevin introduces these concepts and how to use them in their personal and corporate environments. He has taught hundreds in practical leadership in different environments.

Using his extensive experience in the management of organisations and leading people, he designs and implements initiatives and helps lead people to the application of these skills.

Kevin is an author, trainer and international speaker.

wkwconsultingllc.com
www.linkedin.com/in/w-kevin-ward-speaker-messenger

Jamal Ahmed

Jamal Ahmed is an influential Privacy Consultant, strategist, board advisor and Fellow of Information Privacy. He is a leader and innovator in the privacy sector, directing complex Global Privacy Programmes.

He is a sought-after commentator contributing to the BBC and ITV News amongst others, *The Independent* and *The Guardian*. His Privacy Pros Podcast reaches audiences in 100+ countries, is ranked the No 1 privacy podcast globally and is one of the top GDPR podcasts.

Jamal works across multiple sectors and jurisdictions, partnering with boards and C-Suite teams. Alongside exceptional experience and qualifications, he provides pertinent insights, brings alternative perspectives and triggers healthy debate.

Jamal also enjoys his philanthropic work, such as driving supplies to refugees. A family man, Jamal also loves to spend precious time with his wife Rahena and their daughter, Amy.

www.linkedin.com/in/kmjahmed
Twitter: @JamalKazient

Mark Stephen Pooler

Mark runs TMSP Agency, his own PR and digital marketing agency, helping high-profile entrepreneurs share their stories through the use of PR and digital media to become known globally.

In addition, Mark is the Founder, Editor-in-Chief and Media & News Publisher of *MSP News Global,* where he oversees the company's media business as well as its intersection with global business leaders. *MSP News Global* is a premium business magazine website that features influential business leaders, trendsetters and change innovators. Publishing original articles on entrepreneur authors, real estate, coaching, business and many more topics, its headquarters is located in the West Midlands, UK.

Mark is also a professional speaker, international bestselling author and radio host. When not working with his valued clients, Mark enjoys spending time with Lilly, his four-legged bestie!

www.linkedin.com/in/mark-stephen-pooler

Adam Greenwood

Adam Greenwell is a New Zealand-based published author, blogger and columnist, whose long-term goals included writing a book, recording music and the initiative to bring about an improved social condition. He achieved these goals decades ago.

He has a degree in Social Anthropology from Massey University, Palmerston North New Zealand. In 2020, he donated a family papal medal to the City of Palmerston North, now on public display in the Heritage area of the Palmerston North City Library. The Archive includes photographs, such as Adam presenting the medal to Mayor Grant Smith, and many documents on his music project *Get Some Vision - a Tribute to Leonardo da Vinci* (1998).

With his world-class skills as a connector, he formed Adam Greenwell Agency in 2020 to introduce global businesses and projects in and from New Zealand.

www.linkedin.com/in/adam-greenwell-95404217
Twitter: @towngreenmusic

Sam Dossa

Father, husband, mental health advocate, Emotional Intelligence catalyst, mentor, business and personal coach, relationship coach and founder of MenTell Health®.

Proud father of three beautiful daughters. I have carved myself with authenticity, integrity, self-care, self-respect, self-love and a strong connection with self. I have built within me the purity of happiness.

I have been immersed in personal motivation and permanent transformation, starting as a coach in the Youth Sector. As a result of my extensive international training of entrepreneurs and leaders since 2002, I am recognised as one of the UK's top trainers and coaches.

In 2005, I started giving talks and workshops for young adults at schools and colleges, and have since trained 8,000 young adults. Within the corporate environment, I have delivered training on mindfulness, meditation, mental health, communication skills, listening skills, team building, emotional intelligence and bespoke training.

www.linktree.com/Coachsamuk

Simon Alexander Ong

Simon Alexander Ong is a personal development entrepreneur, coach and public speaker. His clients are from all walks of life but they share one trait; they all believe that the greatest investment you can make is in yourself. Simon has been interview by Sky News and BBC, while Barclays featured him in a nationwide campaign asking him questions on how families could embrace better lifestyle habits.

Simon has featured in *HuffPost*, *Forbes*, *Virgin* and *The Guardian*. He also regularly speaks at organisations including Salesforce, Microsoft, EY, Adobe and Unilever, and global keynotes public events and conferences.

His debut book *Energize* was published by Penguin in April 2022 and became an instant bestseller. It also received endorsements from the likes of *New York Times* bestselling authors Simon Sinek, Marie Forleo and Dr Marshall Goldsmith.

www.linkedin.com/in/simonalexanderong
Twitter: @SimonAlexanderO
www.instagram.com/simonalexandero

Brenda Dempsey

Brenda Dempsey is an award-winning entrepreneur, philanthropist and publisher. As a Master Coach, she enables people to accelerate their potential and achieve their goals and dreams.

Brenda is a bestselling author and a woman of influence, and was voted Woman Leader to Look Up To in 2022. She is also the Chief Strategic Officer (CSO) of the International Institute of Influencers, the Vice President of the International House of Speakers, and an Advisory Board member of Africa and Asia Chamber of Commerce.

Having a prominent and highly successful career as a teacher and coach, Brenda has a unique and powerful skillset that has enabled her to consistently facilitate the success and growth of others in many industries and countries around the world.

www.linkedin.com/in/brendadempsey
bookbrilliancepublishing.com
linktr.ee/BrendaDempsey

Acknowledgements

I appreciate the 17 men who found the courage to be themselves in a changing world and become the beacons of light and brilliance for the world to see and follow.

I am grateful to the men who have taught me many lessons and walked a path of strength, resilience and courage.

Thank you to the male authors I have worked with who have learned the power of vulnerability, been open to discussions and transformed their lives so they can empower others. You are my teachers.

In loving memory of my late father and hero, from whom I have inherited love, joy and belief in the power of connection and family.

My eternal gratitude to the Book Brilliance Publishing team, who tirelessly work to produce high-quality books with soul.